Lucas Grollenberg

A Bible for Our Time

Reading the Bible in the light of
today's questions

SCM PRESS LTD

06/20

Translated by John Bowden from the Dutch
Modern bijbellezen
published by Uitgeverij Bosch & Keuning n.v., Baarn
Fifth printing 1977
© Bosch & Keuning n.v. 1971

334 00108 0

British edition first published 1979
by SCM Press Ltd
58 Bloomsbury Street London WC1

Filmset in Monophoto Ehrhardt 10 on 11½ pt by
Richard Clay (The Chaucer Press) Ltd, Bungay, Suffolk
and printed in Great Britain by Fletcher & Son Ltd, Norwich

Contents

Preface to the British Edition

During my theological training I often heard the expression *Catholica non leguntur* – books by Roman Catholics on questions of faith and life are not read outside their own circle. I usually felt that the phrase had connotations of peevishness and pique: we Catholics have the truth; we form a closed circle of like-minded people and that is why outsiders will not listen to us, no matter how loudly or clearly we proclaim our truth.

After the Second World War things changed. Catholics became freer to subject the content of their faith, including the Bible, to historical criticism. As they did so, they began to collaborate more and more with non-Catholics. When I wrote a non-technical account of the historical approach to the Bible in 1968, it was published by a firm which was not exclusively Catholic, and was immediately read and welcomed by Protestants and Catholics alike. Consequently the editors of a Dutch series called Oekumene asked me to write a short book which would show why and how this modern approach to the Bible could bring Christians from the different denominations closer to one another. The book appeared in the series in 1971 under the title *Modern bijbellezen*.

SCM Press have recently published the first book I mentioned under the title *Rediscovering the Bible*. I am glad that they have now decided to publish the Oekumene book as well, in John Bowden's translation. It follows a simple pattern. I begin, in chapter I, by describing how the traditional concept of inspiration arose and how it has functioned over the centuries. This will show why there was so much resistance to modern historical criticism in the churches (chapter II). Finally, in chapter III I discuss the dilemma in which many

Christians find themselves and try to show what seems to me to be the best way out of it.

I found myself discussing one part of this book, namely the section about the person of Jesus in chapter I, with a great many people. The result of these conversations appeared in the Oekumene series in 1974 as a book on Jesus. That book led me on to try to discuss Paul's interpretation of Jesus on the basis of his authentic letters. This resulted in a book on Paul which was published in 1977. John Bowden has already translated both these books and they have been published by SCM Press. I hope that no one will take it amiss that I repeat myself once or twice in these different books. I am not inventive enough always to be original, certainly not when dealing with subjects which are so closely connected.

Lucas Grollenberg OP
Nijmegen, 1978

I · Inspired Books and Their Interpretation

'The first thing that God created was a pen. The pen asked, "What must I do?" God answered, "Write!" The pen said, "What must I write?" Then God said, "Write what is going to happen to everything, right down to the last day."'

In this story, God is Allah. It is about the Muslim holy book, the Koran.[1] In fact this book came into being by stages. Shortly after the year 610, Mohammed began to call upon his fellow-citizens in Mecca to repent. The end of the world was near. The prophet claimed that the angel Gabriel had appeared to tell him this. Some of the 'revelations' recited by Mohammed were already written down in his lifetime, and soon after his death, in 632, disciples collected his sayings, whether remembered or recorded, in a book, '*the* book' of the Muslims. This quickly came to be regarded as a great miracle of Allah, and as a proof of Mohammed's divine mission.

People expressed this reverence for the Koran by attributing the book directly to God, as in the story above. The Koran must have existed before all other things. Islamic thinkers even argued that the Koran is eternal and uncreated, because this book is the utterance of God himself. Everything that is God's is eternal, even his words, and so the Koran is, too . . .

A similar argument had already been developed in Judaism. Experts in other religions and other cultures point to similar phenomena there. Whenever a community begins to venerate a particular writing as a holy book, two things usually happen. Those who actually wrote the text are quickly forgotten, or at least fade from sight. They seem to be outshone by the divine light which the written words shed upon believers. The words are seen to be God's own words and the origin of the book is set in the divine world. If the human writer is still allowed a place, he is thought to be 'inspired'; what he wrote was 'breathed into' him ('inspiration' means 'in-breathing') from above, or was dictated to him by a heavenly voice, or he copied it from a heavenly text which was shown to him in visions.

This is one thing that happens when a text is said to be divine. Another is that from then on, no one is allowed to change anything in it. The 'letter' is fixed once and for all. However, like anything in our world, the community in which the holy book is used is subject to change. There are changes in society, new insights gain accept-ance, old customs give place to new. If they are to be accepted by the community of believers, all these new developments must be covered by divine authority. Everything must be found written in the holy book. And so we have a further phenomenon: a way of interpreting the holy scripture develops which changes with the times, and which in each successive period defines the 'spirit' in which the 'letter' must be understood.

In this chapter we shall keep to the history of the books which have been claimed as holy scripture in the Jewish and Christian communities. You may well come across expressions and 'explana-tions' which surprise you; you may even think them foolish or ridi-culous at first sight. To do so, however, would be a pity. The be-lievers of ancient times whom we shall meet in this chapter were neither more foolish nor more unreasonable than we are. It is just that they thought about things in a different way; they had different ways of expressing their ideas and feelings about what it is to be a human being.

1. Judaism and its holy book

Writing was well established in Israel by the time of David and Solomon, but the Israelites did not yet have a generally accepted holy book. The art of writing held the same place within Israel as within any other developed society. The need for as it were a profes-sional civil service in the new kingdom which David established was one important stimulus. This new kingdom combined Judah in the south, over which David already reigned, with the rest of Israel, which had previously given allegiance to the house of Saul. To organize taxation and military service David held a census. Records had to be made of everyone. To set them up, David had recourse to trained officials from abroad, above all from Egypt. He also sent people from Judah there to be trained in specific jobs. In this way the new capital, Jerusalem, quickly acquired a large number of educated men, including professional scribes. Among the clerks and secretaries were those who appreciated literature and even produced it themselves, in Hebrew. The author of the attractive story of Joseph's adventures in Egypt probably had a background of this kind. The reign of Solomon, David's son and successor, is seen as the first golden age of Hebrew literature. One classic from this period is the story of how Solomon came to be born and of the political complications which developed before he succeeded to his father's throne. This marvellous piece of literature has survived because it came to be included in the Bible (II Sam. 9–20, continued and concluded in I Kings 1–2). When it was written, however, it was just one more piece of literature. The same is true of a more obviously religious work, by the writer known as the Yahwist: we shall hear more of him in chapter III.

In many Israelite sanctuaries, in larger and smaller temples, writings of a religious kind were preserved and used; there were texts with sacred narratives, descriptions of rites and liturgical songs. However, these did not have the status of holy books which governed the life of a whole community.

The situation did not change after Solomon's death (about 930 BC), when the kingdom split into two parts, the large northern state of Israel and the smaller state of Judah with its capital, Jerusalem. In these societies all sorts of things were written down on a variety of materials. There were bills and short messages, on broken bits of pottery; letters, contracts, reports, annals and pieces of literature on sheets of papyrus which were imported from Egypt. Those who were rich enough to afford it wrote on treated animal skins, parchment. Inks of various kinds were available. These writing materials were also used by priests attached to sanctuaries, not only national temples like those of Jerusalem in the south and Bethel and Dan in the north, but also those in other places. It is certain that the prophets Elijah and Elisha were familiar with traditions from Israel's past, some of which may also have been written down. These will have included both stories about the patriarchs and the exodus from Egypt and collections of laws and regulations.

In 721 BC the state of Israel was invaded by the Assyrians and swept off the map. The Assyrians deported the members of the ruling classes, scattering them over their vast empire, and replaced them with colonists from Assyria. The newcomers, of course, brought their gods and priests and rites with them. It is almost certain that at this time a number of faithful worshippers of Yahweh, Israel's God, who maintained Israel's earliest traditions, sought refuge in Judah and took these traditions with them, perhaps even in written form. How they established them in the south we do not know, but a century later king Josiah profited from their zeal. When the Assyrian empire began to collapse, Josiah (who reigned from 640 to 609 BC, or thereabouts) planned to restore the nation to its former greatness. This also meant a thoroughgoing reformation of the national religion. The Temple in Jerusalem, which in earlier years had been defaced and desecrated by all kinds of additions from other religions, was thoroughly purified and restored. In the process, a law book was found which went back to ancient traditions, evidently the work of people who had come from what was once the heart of the country, the area around Shechem. King Josiah based his reforms on this text, which seems to have been something like the nucleus of the book of Deuteronomy in our Bible (chapters 12–26). The people of Judah were to rediscover their true unity, their 'identity', by worshipping their one God together at only one place, the Temple in Jerusalem. In this way, Josiah breathed new life into the ancient notion of the 'covenant'. He was helped in his task by all kinds of 'wise men', with some knowledge of the past, who had access to archives and could write. They collected a variety of documents together to form a kind of historical work, rather like a national epic. They put the newly discovered law book, which bore Moses' name, in a setting of addresses and 'sermons' given by Moses. He promised prosperity if the people lived in faithful observance of his laws and ordinances, and threatened terrible disasters and utter destruction if they forgot their covenant with Yahweh. They used this work as a preface to the 'history' which we know from the books of Joshua, Judges, Samuel and Kings. In these books they arranged, revised and supplemented the material at their disposal in such a way that it showed the reader quite clearly how the principles laid down by 'Moses', the blessing and the curse, had been at work through this history.

Even then, the great work could not yet become 'holy scripture'. The necessary conditions for this had yet to develop. Religion was one of the many expressions of the life of a community ruled over by a king, with an army, diplomats, agriculture, industry and commerce. The Babylonians were soon to put an end to this thriving life. They had taken over the declining Assyrian empire and now Egypt seemed an attractive direction in which to turn their forces. In 597 BC they captured Jerusalem and deported some of the leading classes to Babylon. They would have preferred to allow Judah to continue to exist as a tributary kingdom, but it proved too unreliable. In 587 they totally destroyed it. In so doing they made possible the conditions in which Judaism could develop.

Ezekiel, the priest and prophet, could be regarded as the founder of Judaism. He taught the disillusioned exiles from Judah how to practise their old faith under these new conditions. The rich life of the nation of which this faith had once been a part had now come to an end. However, Yahweh was not bound to land and Temple. Ezekiel had watched the divine glory leaving the Temple and had seen it in the midst of Babylonia. Yahweh was also to be found there. And people could come together by observing rites and customs which did not depend on sacrificial worship offered in one particular place. In Babylon the sabbath acquired a new significance; it became the means of forming a community. Moreover, because circumcision was unknown there, it too served to mark out the male exiles from the Babylonians. For the Judaeans, this again became a symbol of togetherness, a token of the covenant. A third practice which bound the exiles together was their refusal to eat certain foods which were common in Babylonia, because of their belief in Yahweh.

We do not know much about the life of the exiles. It is, however, certain that as they met together week by week, they were concerned with what they had brought with them from the ruins of the city and the Temple: recollections of Israel's past, forms of words in which the faith had once been expressed or even written down. They pondered the threats of various prophets which had been fulfilled. It

5

was clear that what the prophets had said had indeed been words of God. Other inspired authors, like Ezekiel and the man who wrote Isaiah 40–55, added their own oracles. Priests, now freed from their many duties in the Temple, pored over ancient ritual texts and edited them, hoping that one day they might become a new liturgy to be used in Jerusalem, in the new spirit of remorse and repentance. Here we have the beginnings of all kinds of texts which were later to become 'holy scripture'.

With all this, many Judaeans became more and more firmly rooted in Babylonia. When Cyrus conquered Babylon and gave permission to all those who had been deported to return home, taking their gods with them, only a few Judaeans heeded the appeal of their leaders. As a result, the community which came into being in and around Jerusalem had rather a wretched time. As a recent historian put it: 'The new Israel wanted desperately something to draw it together and give it distinctive identity.'[2] The man who fulfilled this need was Ezra. He was a scribe who, on the authority of the Persians, brought to Jerusalem a law book which had been prepared in Babylonia. Unfortunately the exact date is unknown. Some would put it in 398 BC, others prefer 458 or 428. It is, however, certain that the solemn acceptance of the law book by the people, as described in Nehemiah 8, became a turning point. It is sometimes seen as the birth of Judaism, just as Ezra is often seen as the father of Judaism. This even led to a new definition of the concept of Israel. In the words of the historian I quoted earlier

> Israel would no longer be a national entity, nor one coterminous with the descendants of the Israelite tribes or the inhabitants of the old national territory, nor even a community of those who in some way acknowledged Yahweh as God and offered him worship. From now on, Israel would be viewed (as in the theology of the Chronicler) as that remnant of Judah which had rallied round the law. He would be a member of Israel (i.e., a Jew) who assumed the burden of that law.

But this redefinition of Israel meant inevitably the emergence of a religion in which law was central. This betokened, let it be repeated, no break with Israel's ancient faith, all the major features of which continued in force, but a radical regrouping of that faith

6

about the law. The law no longer merely regulated the affairs of an already constituted community; it had created the community!

We do not know for certain whether the law book brought by Ezra was already in the form of the 'five books of Moses', 'the Pentateuch', as it is in our Bible. According to some scholars the Pentateuch as we know it only came into being in the fourth century. Be this as it may, in later centuries we see reverence for the 'holy book' expressed more and more strongly, while at the same time methods were developed to interpret that word of God in terms of the problems and the insights of each particular age.

2. Divine words, written down by Moses

Shortly after 200 BC, a wise teacher in Jerusalem, Jesus son of Sirach, wrote of the divine wisdom which was the real source of all the good that he expressed in his words. Imitating the Book of Proverbs (chapter 8), he portrays Wisdom as a female figure which came forth from God before all things and was with him when he made the universe, heaven and earth, and all the nations on earth. 'Among them all I looked for a home; in whose territory was I to settle?', Lady Wisdom relates. 'Then the Creator of the universe laid a command upon me: "Make your home in . . . Israel." So I came to be established in Jerusalem . . . I grew like a fair olive-tree.'

> I am the mother of fair love,
> Of the fear of God, of knowledge, and of holy hope;
> In me is all the grace of life and truth,
> In me all hope of life and virtue.
> Come to me, you who desire me,
> and eat your fill of my fruit . . .
> To obey me is to be safe from disgrace,
> those who work in wisdom will not go astray.

The writer's comment which follows this rapturous poetry jars somewhat on our sensibility:

> *All this is the covenant-book of God Most High,*
> *the Law which Moses enacted to be the heritage of*
> *the assemblies of Jacob.*

7

For Jesus Sirach the scribe, the Law of Moses is nothing less than eternal Wisdom, which has now become a book.

Another passage, perhaps written somewhat later, comes from the short work which bears the name of Baruch and is usually put in the Greek Bible (and e.g. in the Jerusalem Bible) after Jeremiah and Lamentations. The writer is dealing with a theme which also appears in Job 28: no matter where man may seek, the way to Wisdom is hidden from him:

> No one knows the way to her,
> no one can discover the path she treads.
> But the One who knows all knows her,
> he has grasped her with his own intellect,
> he has set the earth firm for ever
> and filled it with four-footed beasts,
> he sends the light – and it goes,
> he recalls it – and trembling it obeys;
> the stars shine joyfully at their set times:
> when he calls them, they answer, 'Here we are';
> they gladly shine for their creator.
> It is he who is our God,
> no other can compare with him.
> He has grasped the whole way of knowledge,
> and confided it to his servant Jacob,
> to Israel his well-beloved;
> *so causing her to appear on earth*
> *and move among men.*
> *This is the book of the commandments of God,*
> *the Law that stands for ever.*

The poem ends with an exhortation to Israel to live in the light of the Law, to hold it fast and not to give the divine glory to others,

> Israel, blessed are we:
> what pleases God has been revealed to us.[3]

In this way, the idea could also emerge that the Law, the Torah, itself existed with God before all things. It was expressed in all sorts of ways. 'When God said, "Let *us* make man," he was speaking to the Torah.' It was also said that God created the world 'for the sake

8

of the Torah', and the Torah was even regarded as the instrument of creation: the world was created through the Torah. Hence sayings like: 'Anyone who affirms that the Torah does not come from heaven shall have no part in the world to come,' and, 'Anyone who says that Moses wrote even a single line on his own authority is a liar and despises God's word.'[4]

At times, 'Torah' can mean something like 'revelation'. However, in many of the sayings of this kind people are clearly thinking of the Pentateuch. The last lines of the Pentateuch describe the death of Moses. Even these sentences were 'given' to him, whether they were dictated to him or whether he copied them from the heavenly texts that were shown to him.

The idea of a text existing in heaven on heavenly 'tablets' can be found in a writing which was very popular in Jesus' day, at least in some circles. It has many titles, but the best known is 'The Book of Jubilees'. It is a kind of biblical history. In his own way, the writer relates the contents of the book of Genesis and the beginning of Exodus, as far as Sinai. First of all, he is very interested in chronology. He divides the time since creation into periods of forty-nine years, seven times seven, 'jubilees'. On this basis he gives precise dates to each event. After Adam had lived for seven years in Paradise, 'in the second month, on the seventeenth day, the serpent came and approached Eve . . .' We shall come back to this interest in dates later. What concerns us here is what the writer and his audience thought about the Law. Written down on heavenly tablets even before creation, it had been in force from the beginning and would always remain in force. Even the highest angels keep the sabbath with joy, obedient to the most fundamental commandment of the Torah. Once he has left Paradise, Adam presents a fragrant offering of incense every morning, prepared in accordance with Exodus 30.34. Abraham celebrated the Feast of Tabernacles according to the way in which the commandments of the Law were observed in the author's community.

The author leaves out some of the less attractive deeds of the Israelite patriarchs which are recorded in Genesis: the lies told by Abraham and Isaac about their wives, the way in which Jacob deceives Laban, and Jacob's fear of his brother Esau. He even praises some misdeeds. In his view, for example, Simeon and Levi did a praiseworthy work in massacring the population of Shechem; indeed it was because of this act that Levi and his tribe were chosen for the priesthood. The author wants to know nothing of a reconciliation between Jacob and his brother Esau. On the contrary, he has Esau killed by Jacob's own hand. This is in line with what he earlier makes their old, blind father Isaac say to Esau: 'If you throw off his (Jacob's) yoke, you will be committing a mortal sin and your posterity will be blotted out.'[5]

This seems strange to us. On the one hand the Torah is a book written in heaven, and on the other hand the author of Jubilees alters the details of the Genesis stories whenever it suits him. At the root of this contradiction lies an ardent belief in the unique role of 'Israel'. On the basis of this belief, the Law on which the Jewish community is based becomes an absolute, divine entity, and at the same time everything outside this community is rejected (Esau = Edom = the embodiment of whatever is non-Jewish, the Gentiles; Shechem = the Samaritans, who are even worse than the Gentiles). To put it another way: the author is writing from within and on behalf of a community which can maintain its identity only by experiencing a unique bond with the one true God and by an almost fanatical rejection of what 'the world', in fact the brilliant and world-wide culture of Hellenism, has to offer by way of 'wisdom' and universal humanity.

3. An 'inspired' translation

Of course, people thought that the heavenly tablets which Moses copied had been written in Hebrew. That was the language of God and his angels, and of Adam and Eve. But how was the divine law now to be read by Jews who for generations had been living in a Greek-speaking environment and no longer understood the language of the Torah?

This problem first arose in Egypt. People from Judah had emigrated there even before the disaster of 587. After that, others came to join them. We know that some took up military service. Even before the Persian prince Cambyses invaded Egypt (525 BC), there was a military colony on the island of Elephantine in the Nile, near present-day Aswan, which had a garrison of Jewish mercenaries.

There they had built a temple for their God Yahu. Excavations have unearthed letters which suggest that this temple was destroyed in 410 at the instigation of Egyptian priests, and was restored a few years later. These Jews spoke and wrote Aramaic.

From the beginning of the sixth century BC onwards, many colonists from Greece had come to live in the Nile delta, and after Egypt was conquered by Alexander the Great, Greek became more and more the principal language, especially in the rapidly growing capital city which the conqueror had founded and called Alexandria. His successors, the brilliant Ptolemies, did everything possible to make this city the greatest centre of culture and technology in the then known world. In its prime it must have had almost a million inhabitants, including tens of thousands of Jews. They had their own quarter of the city, but many of them lived elsewhere, so that their shops and synagogues were also scattered. As a religious group they had their own governing body, a kind of council of elders, with an ethnarch, a community leader, at their head. They regarded the Jews still living in Palestine as their brethren, and had a deep reverence for Jerusalem and its Temple.

There were also scholars and scribes among the Jews of Alexandria. Ptolemy I had already begun to attract learned men from all over the world, not only writers, but also astronomers, geographers, physicians and historians. He made liberal provision of everything they needed for their scientific investigations. Ptolemy I also laid the foundation for the library at Alexandria which became so famous; in about 235 BC it had 490,000 scrolls. It was possible to find not only the whole of Greek literature there, but also translations of works from Egypt and Babylonia. Even writings from faraway India found their way into this collection, which was the greatest in the world before the invention of printing.

In those conditions it was not difficult to meet the needs of synagogue worshippers and to replace the more or less spontaneous translations of passages from the Torah with a generally approved Greek text of the whole of the divine work of Moses. It was a genuine translation, in the sense that the meaning of the Hebrew text was rendered in the thought-patterns of the translators. To take one example which has recently been used in a discussion of abortion: an ancient law in the book of Exodus deals with a case in which a pregnant woman gets involved in a fight between two men and suffers a blow which causes a miscarriage. The Hebrew text is not entirely clear, but it seems to say that if the blow is not fatal to the woman, the one who struck her can make amends with a fine; if, however, she dies, then it has to be 'a life for a life'. The translator is more interested in the dead child. So in the Greek, Moses decrees: 'If her child comes forth not yet formed, he (the one who struck the blow) shall pay a fine . . .; but if it was formed, he shall pay his life for the life . . .' (The decision as to whether or not the child was formed would be made in accordance with the scientific views of the time: the male foetus was formed after forty days and the female after ninety.)[6]

This, then, was a genuine 'translation'. But a great many Jews still had difficulty with it. Should the wisdom which God had granted only to Israel now simply be made accessible to outsiders, to Gentiles? Could it be reproduced in a language which in fact had no connection with the revelation? In order to counter these difficulties, in the course of the second century BC an Alexandrian Jew wrote the little book which has come down to us under the title 'The Letter of Aristeas'.[7]

The writer tells a certain Philocrates how he was sent by king Ptolemy (305–282) to the high priest in Jerusalem to discuss a translation of the Law. Aristeas himself had been present when the chief librarian in Alexandria had informed the king that there was a Jewish book in Jerusalem, written on parchment in Hebrew letters, which also needed to be made available in Greek. After a digression about Jewish captives who were freed through his intervention, Aristeas describes how he and another high official named Andreas came to the high priest Eleazar. They put before him the king's request that he should send a number of translators, who were to be both upright and knowledgeable, to Egypt with a copy of the Hebrew Law. The high priest accepted the valuable presents which the king had sent, and chose six scribes from each of the twelve tribes who were well acquainted with Greek language and culture. After he had had a long discussion with them about the meaning of the prohibition against eating certain animals, Aristeas left for Alexandria with the chosen translators. Contrary to standard protocol – which prescribed a waiting period of several days – the guests were received immediately by the great king. He prostrated himself seven times before the sacred text, saw that his guests were properly lodged, and then gave a banquet in their honour which lasted for seven days. Every day the ruler questioned ten of his guests about the tasks and obligations of a king, who according to Hellenistic ideals was expected to be a virtuous and wise man. The chosen translators seemed to be miraculously well informed on these matters. 'Aristeas' reports all their wise answers. After three days, the seventy-two translators set to work on a peaceful island, and 'it happened that the task of translation was completed in exactly seventy-two days, as though a precise time limit had been set for it.' The text was read aloud in the presence of the Jewish community and was given enthusiastic approval. From now on, this was to be the text of the Torah, and not a single letter of it could be altered. The writer goes on to relate how people who had used passages from the Torah in their own translations were punished for this by God, with mental disorders and blindness. Finally the translators returned to Jerusalem under royal escort, laden with gifts for the high priest.

This provided reassurance for the synagogue worshippers. The Greek text in general use was the best translation imaginable, made under the patronage of the great Ptolemy, by scholars from all the tribes of Israel who had been chosen by the high priest himself; they worked in Alexandria, the best possible setting, peaceful and scholarly, where they miraculously completed their work in seventy-two days.

The story served its purposes beautifully. This is clear from the way in which it was elaborated as time went on. Philo, the great Jewish philosopher (about 13 BC to AD 45), tells it in his own way, with even more miraculous features. The high priest of Jerusalem, who is now also 'king' of the Jews, sees the request of Ptolemy, the greatest ruler of all times, as a clear sign from God. The seventy-two translators prepare for their work on the island of Pharos with intense prayer, and then begin to write under divine inspiration. Each of them makes his own translation of the entire Law, and comparing their texts when they have finished, they find that all seventy-two agree with one another word for word. Given the large vocabulary of Greek, Philo remarks, it is clear that these men did not work merely as scholars; the words were 'breathed into each of them

13

as by the same invisible prompter'. Indeed, they were not translators, but hierophants (priests who disclose divine mysteries) and prophets. Philo goes on to describe how at that time a festival was instituted, to be celebrated annually on the island, commemorating the miracle of the translation which had been made there.

It would also be possible to make an anthology of early Christian writers who took over the story with all sorts of variants and ornamentations. We can understand how this happened: the Greek translation of the Jewish scriptures was essential for Christians; they used this text to 'prove' the divine truth of their new faith. However, for this very reason the 'Septuagint'[8] (i.e. translation made by the 'seventy') quickly fell into disuse among the Jews. The Jews had much more literal translations of the Hebrew Torah made so as to strengthen their position in arguments with the Christians. In the end, they abandoned the Greek translations altogether. Thus it came about that the annual festival in honour of the Septuagint became a Jewish day of fasting and repentance, a recollection of the disastrous moment at which the divine Torah was delivered over to unbelievers.

4. Methods of interpretation

The Jews acknowledged two other collections of writings as sacred, in addition to the Torah, which was quickly divided up into five books. These were 'the prophets' and 'the writings', and they soon came to share in the sacred character of the Torah. They too came from God, and the writers were compared with Moses: all of them were 'inspired'. Joshua, the successor whom Moses had appointed at God's command, was close enough to that original source of all inspiration to qualify as the author of the book of which he himself was the hero and which came to bear his name, the book of Joshua. The great prophet Samuel had written the book of Judges and the work which followed it and was named after him. Jeremiah was thought to be the author of Kings. The so-called 'later' prophets were each written by the divine spokesmen after which they were named: the books of Isaiah, Jeremiah, Ezekiel and the Twelve (the minor prophets). The various 'writings' also came from inspired men. The wisdom which Solomon set down in Proverbs and

Ecclesiastes had been imparted to him by God himself, in answer to his prayer. David, who was changed into a new person by the spirit of God, was the inspired author of the book of Psalms. In fact this book contained all sorts of liturgical poems which had been composed over the centuries, combined into groups, and finally, about 250 BC, had been given fixed form in the Psalter which divided the 150 psalms into five books, like the Torah. However, their historical origin was quickly forgotten to make room for the conviction that David was the inspired author of the book of Psalms. When the 150 psalms were collected in a single book, seventy-three of them already bore David's name. The superscriptions of some of them even described the circumstances in which the psalm was thought to have been composed, 'when the prophet Nathan came to him after he had gone in to Bathsheba' (Ps. 51), and 'when he sat in the cave, when he was fleeing from Saul' (Ps. 57). This conviction was expressed even more strongly in the Greek translation of the book: there David's name is attached to eighty-four psalms, and a 151st psalm is added under the title: 'Written by David himself when he fought with Goliath'.

However, in none of these cases is the 'inspiration' as complete as it is with the Torah. For the Torah, the principle holds that everything is included in the divine Law. If its text existed before all things, if the Torah was the instrument of creation, and if its words are to remain even when earth and heaven have passed away, then this principle is a reasonable one. That means: first, that everything that can be known about the world and what happens in it must be contained in the text. Secondly, it must contain all the true wisdom of all times, and no letter or sign in it can be without profound significance. Thirdly, a person might devote a whole lifetime to developing and applying methods which seek to extract from the divine text an insight into the mysteries of human life and the world.

This view is still held in our own day. In 1963, a book was published in The Hague under the title *The Bible as Creation*.[9] The word 'Bible' in the title does not refer here to the book usually described in the Christian world in these terms, i.e. the whole of the Old and New Testaments, but only to the Torah. The author, F. Weinreb, was convinced of the divine origin of the Torah: it had come into being in the way described above. It had to be possible to discover the order of creation in the text: all the secrets of the cosmos and of human life were contained in it. Of course, the real and most profound meanings did not emerge on an ordinary reading of the text; a key had to be found. Weinreb claimed to possess this key, which had been handed down to him from generation to generation through Jewish groups.

The key was that each letter of the Hebrew alphabet also had a numerical value: *aleph* stood for 1, *beth* for 2, *gimel* for 3, and so on. By calculating the value of certain words in the narratives of the Torah it was possible to discover miraculous correlations. The Hebrew word for the 'mist' which, according to the creation narrative (Gen. 2.6), arose from the earth consists of two letters with the values 1 and 4. The four rivers of Paradise thus flow from this mist. The word for 'man', consisting of three letters, with values of 1, 4 and 40, had the same structure. The human situation is also marked by the number four: the letters of 'the tree of the knowledge of good and evil', totalling 932, have exactly four times the value of the 'tree of life', totalling 233.

According to this interpretation, what seems to the reader to be an ordinary historical account in fact has much deeper meanings. For example, Abraham pitched his tent between Bethel and Ai (Gen. 12.8). If we subtract 'Ai' from 'Bethel', the result is 358, which is also the value of the word 'Messiah'. Moreover, when the tent stood half way between these two places, the distance was half of 358, i.e. 179, which is the value of Paradise, 'the garden of Eden'. Weinreb concludes: 'In fact, after this life of making a mockery of idols and shattering them, Abraham comes to the place which is the garden of Eden, on the way which is the way of the Messiah.'

Weinreb's book is almost 600 pages long, but he claims that he has given only a small sample of all the mysteries that can be discovered in the Torah in this way. The presupposition of his method is that the text was fixed by God in the very beginning. On this basis, Weinreb can write: 'Therefore not a jot or a tittle in the Bible may be changed. Were that to happen, the whole structure would collapse. And in that case we would be left with nothing more than a "story".'

Even before the beginning of the Christian era, Jewish scribes were speculating with the help of the numerical value of Hebrew

16

letters and words, and traces of this approach can be found in the sacred books themselves. As far as our subject is concerned, Weinreb's presupposition is particularly important: the Torah is of divine origin, and therefore contains all knowledge. Moreover, deeper matters must also lie concealed in texts which at first glance are far from profound, which seem pedestrian, contain contradictions or in one way or another are unworthy of God. It is obvious that here the standards of the reader, the interpreter and their community are paramount. What they expect of a book written by God must be found in it.

To take an example from the Letter of Aristeas, mentioned above: Aristeas describes how he had a conversation in Jerusalem about certain regulations in the divine law. He repeats this at length as part of his defence of the Jewish way of life against objections raised from a 'common sense' perspective, as this was understood in Alexandria at that time. The high priest said:

> Now our Lawgiver being a wise man and specially endowed by God to understand all things, took a comprehensive view of each particular detail, and fenced us round with impregnable ramparts and walls of iron, that we might not mingle at all with any of the other nations, but remain pure in body and soul, free from all vain imaginations, worshipping the one Almighty God above the whole creation.[10]

He goes on to explain why the network of prescriptions with which God has surrounded the Jews, his true servants, also contains regulations about the eating of animals. In the laws of Leviticus 11 and Deuteronomy 14, Moses was not in fact concerned with weasels and rats. He was concerned simply with morality. It should be noted that the birds which may be eaten are tame and clean, because they feed on seed and green things: they include doves, partridges and geese. Wild and savage birds are prohibited because they transgress the Law and feed on domestic animals, even seizing lambs and kids. Indeed, sometimes they attack men, dead or alive. In prohibiting these birds of prey, Moses wanted to impress on us that we 'must be just and effect nothing by violence, and refrain from relying on our own strength.' Characteristics of animals mentioned in the Law, like divided hoofs or rumination, are also meant in a moral sense; Moses is advising men to avoid bad company and constantly to reflect, 'ruminate' on the great deeds which God has wrought for his people.

Here we approach the world of the great Jewish philosopher Philo. We have already seen that for him the Greek translation of the Torah was not only authoritative but inspired, word by word and even letter by letter. This conviction was connected with his way of doing philosophy. He was steeped in an intellectual world in which various strains of Greek thought, deriving from Plato, the Stoa and the Pythagoreans, came together and influenced one another. As a Jew, Philo wanted to find confirmation in his holy scripture for the true insights which he extracted from this mixture. He was not a pioneer, for in the Greek world, too, there were ancient texts which were thought to be inspired. Had not Homer often invoked the muse? Other poets, too, were guided in their writing by divine powers. Trained philosophers, however, found it difficult to see how the crude and sometimes coarse stories of gods and men in these ancient poems could be meant to be understood literally. For them it stood to reason that divine inspiration had concealed deep philosophical insights under these crude forms, both the barbarous and sensual adventures of the Greek heroes and the verses in which they were described. Verses, after all, are by nature obscure, and are therefore a lower form than rigorous philosophical treatises. Thus in Philo's world, there were all kinds of ways of discovering the real meaning of inspired texts. For Philo, of course, only one text could claim to be inspired, and that was the Torah, passed on to Moses, the greatest of all philosophers, by the one true God himself, and translated into Greek through the inspiration of this same God.

When Moses writes, 'Cain went out from the face of God', he cannot mean precisely what he says. The Existent Being has no face. If this Being had a face, he would have to have a body, with internal and external organs, and the passions and experiences that go with them. Besides, where could Cain go to escape from God? God fills everything that exists.

The only thing left for us to do is to make up our minds that none of the propositions put forward is literally intended and to take

18

the path of figurative interpretation so dear to philosophical souls.[11]

After this, Philo goes on to deal with the scriptural quotations in his usual way: he interprets them with reference to conditions and situations of 'the soul', which is not only the principle of virtue and sin, but the element in man which can have a relationship with God and as a result can undergo all kinds of developments. What the Torah says about the patriarchs points to the kind of spiritual adventures experienced by the soul in its ascent towards a mystical union with God. Abraham's migrations are a sign of the first stage of this ascent. Relying on faith, he leaves behind the land of the Chaldaeans, i.e. the world of material bodies, then quits the world of sensual perception and finally that of rational understanding. Hagar is science that has to be learned; Abraham's true spouse is Sarah, the knowledge of revelation. Jacob's career is the second stage in this spiritual ascent. His wrestling is a struggle against passions; after it he is given the name Israel, the one who sees God. The third stage is the life of Isaac, the laughing one, whose joy is complete. He has God as his father and marries the virgin Rebecca, symbol of the infused knowledge of God, so that he has no need of slave women and concubines, that is, of other sciences.[12]

Where Philo, in the numerous works which have come down to us, follows the Greek text of the Bible, there are all sorts of details which point him to the hidden meanings: the use of a particular preposition, the repetition of a word, the etymology of a Greek term, a word which in strict logic is superfluous, and so on. Moreover, he speculates in some detail about the significance of biblical names, and even about the implication of numbers which appear in the text. The speculations prompted by the fact that there are two accounts of the creation of man are very well known. In Genesis 1.26 God makes man in his own image and likeness, and in 2.7 he forms Adam out of clay and breathes life into him. Thus, two men are made, a heavenly man, who according to Philo is an 'idea', incorporeal, asexual and immortal, and an earthly man, the forefather of the human race.

All this may seem strange to us. Yet Philo was by no means unique in the Judaism of his time, either in his ideas and speculations or in his handling of the biblical text. Jewish scribes in

Palestine pursued similar courses, using the Hebrew Torah and the two other groups of sacred books. One expert on Philo, who summarized his method of scriptural exposition in twenty-three rules, noted that most of them were also applied by the rabbis in Palestine.[13]

We can say more about the interpretation of the Bible in Palestine at the time of Jesus. First of all there was 'the tradition of the elders'. The book of the divine Torah incorporated collections of laws from very different periods. The earliest of them went back to the time before the Israelite monarchy. The complex which forms the nucleus of Deuteronomy acquired its force in the time of king Josiah, as we have already seen. Now it is usually the case with a law book that customs already in vogue are accepted by the lawgiver as generally valid, and thus acquire the 'force of law'. But a community is a living thing, and thus is constantly subject to change. Consequently, after years, or centuries, it comes to need a new law book. By its very nature, the Torah was a long way from covering all the aspects of the daily life of the Jews, even when it was canonized. The demands of the divine lawgiver in a number of activities and circumstances were by no means clear. To discover what was right, it was necessary to inquire of an authoritative interpreter of the Torah. Thus there arose alongside the sacred book a 'tradition' of rules of conduct, a kind of oral interpretation of God's will, a 'Torah' which in Jesus' day commanded an authority equal to that of the written Law. At least this was the case in the circles of the Pharisees, who wanted to make the fulfilling of God's will the characteristic of all the members of the Jewish nation. People liked to say that these oral explanations and expansions of the Torah also went back to Moses himself. He had entrusted them to Joshua, who in turn handed them on to the 'oldest who survived him'. They then gave them to the prophets, who gave them to 'the men of the great synagogue', in the time of Ezra.

In addition to all this, in some circles a very special kind of literature was developed. The canonization of the Torah and, not long afterwards, of other ancient books as well, was a problem for writers who still had something to say to the Jewish community. The time of the prophets was past, according to the official position, and what the faithful were to do and to permit was fixed in the Torah from all eternity and for all ages to come. In the meantime, however, still more disturbing things happened. Breaches were being made in the wall which was being so carefully built around the Law. In the third century BC, Greek culture began irresistibly to penetrate the Jewish community. And now the godless Antiochus began to use brute force to sweep away all the distinguishing features of Judaism: Jewish worship and the Jewish way of life were at risk, and the Law, with the wall that surrounded it, was in danger of being swept away. This was indeed the limit, the end! In former times, in such disasters God had raised up prophets to show the meaning of what was happening. Now a similar spirit drove men to write. Their books are called 'revelation literature' or, to use a word derived from the Greek, 'apocalyptic' books. These writers usually chose a figure from biblical antiquity and showed how God had revealed to him everything that would happen in the future, including, of course, the events of the turbulent time of the writer himself, and what would happen immediately after those events. A good candidate from the past was Enoch, the seventh patriarch after Adam, who had walked with God on earth and at the age of 365 was caught up into heaven without having to die. Moses, too, was a suitable person for giving his people a vision of the future. Baruch, who had experienced the first destruction of Jerusalem and had recorded the visions of Jeremiah, must himself also have received visions about the future crisis for the city. Furthermore, it was said that a wise and pious man named Daniel had lived at the court of Babylon during the exile. He too was a figure to whom God could have revealed something of the fearful years which his people would endure under the wrath of the godless ruler, and something also of the new and eternal kingdom which he would establish immediately after these woes. Those who had died for God's good cause would have a share in that kingdom, and would shine there like stars in the heavens.

In Jesus' day a great many of these 'apocalyptic' books were in circulation. Perhaps they were only read by a few, but the expectations expressed in them were to be found at almost every level of the population. Daniel was the only book from this varied literature to be canonized. When the Romans destroyed Jerusalem and its Temple in AD 70, Judaism discovered new patterns of life under the exclusive leadership of the Pharisees. These fixed the number of

21

sacred books for all time at twenty-four, and rejected the apocalyptic literature. Except for Daniel, therefore, these books fell into disuse among the Jews. As a result, the original Hebrew and Aramaic texts were lost for ever. A number of the books were still read (in translation, of course) in some Christian circles, until they fell into disuse there also. Only in the past century have a number of the lost works come to light again in 'fringe churches', like that of Ethiopia (including the Book of Jubilees, which we have already met).

One apocalyptic book, however, continued to be read with pleasure by Christians for centuries in almost all churches.[14] The author of the book presents himself as Ezra, the great father of Judaism. This Ezra is supposed to be writing in Babylon, thirty years after the first destruction of Jerusalem, i.e. in 557 BC. Ezra describes seven 'visions'. In a way which can still move a modern reader, he raises questions of religious belief: about the power of evil, to which God allows such freedom, and about the riddles posed by God's rule over the world, in which the people of his pleasure receive so little recognition.

At the end, in the seventh 'vision', the author makes an attempt to have his book and other apocalyptic books recognized in the Jewish community, which is in the process of doing away with them. For he is writing about AD 100, thirty years after the destruction of Jerusalem by the Romans in AD 70. It is worthwhile summarizing his story here, first and foremost because for centuries Christians regarded it as a factual account of the actions of the historical Ezra in 557 BC. In addition to this, however, it also shows how a Jewish writer from the earliest Christian period can conceive of 'inspiration', as a consequence of his desire to provide a foundation for the authority of a writing. Ezra hears a voice saying, 'Open your mouth and drink what I give you.' He sees a cup being handed to him, with a drink which looks like water but has the colour of fire. He drinks, and then feels his heart filled with knowledge, his breast with wisdom and his mind with memory. This experience comes to him while he is in voluntary seclusion from the community, having simply taken five competent secretaries with him. In a state of ecstasy he begins to dictate to them, and keeps this up for forty days and forty nights. First he dictates the text of the twenty-four sacred books of the Jews which had been lost at the destruction of

Jerusalem (NB, the destruction of 587!), and then seventy others. He has to make the first twenty-four public, so that they can be read by worthy and unworthy people alike; the other seventy (meaning the 'apocalyptic' books) are to be restricted to the wise men among the people.

In conclusion, something should be said about biblical interpretation among the 'Essenes', a group of Jesus' contemporaries who had separated themselves from this evil world and all its 'children of darkness' in order to wait in the wilderness by the Dead Sea for the great events which would put an end to the dominion of evil. These 'children of light' saw their group as 'the community of the new covenant'. Among the finds made since 1947 in the ruins of their settlement and particularly in caves in the cliffs nearby have been fragments of their biblical commentaries. A special method is used in them. A couple of lines from the Bible are quoted, followed by the words, 'Interpreted, this means . . .' The word for 'interpreted', *pesher*, is evidently a technical term; it appears in chapters 2, 4, 5 and 7 of Daniel in our Bible. There it signifies the 'interpretation' of something mysterious, something that comes from God, like Nebudchadnezzar's dreams, the sudden writing on the wall of the palace at Belshazzar's feast, or the four monsters which come out of the sea. Only through a kind of divine inspiration can Daniel or the angel explain the meaning of the vision for the present day.

For the community by the Dead Sea, this is obviously also the case with the text of the Bible. It comes from God and must have a meaning for the present day. For that present is the great fulfilment of history for which all earlier ages have looked and about which the prophets and psalmists wrote in mysterious words. The community itself has a key position in these decisive events: it is the chosen flock of the children of light through which God will destroy all the wickedness in this world. In the texts which have been discovered, the founder of the group is referred to as the 'Teacher of Righteousness' and is nowhere mentioned by name. He must have lived in the time of the Maccabees – either Jonathan (160–143 BC) or more probably Simon (143–134 BC). The latter must have been the 'godless priest' who made it impossible for the 'Teacher of Righteousness' to live in Jerusalem and who drove him and his followers into the wilderness. The practice of interpreting the biblical texts in terms of the fortunes of the community goes back to him.

In the commentary on Habakkuk (the end of 2.2), the following passage appears (the biblical text is printed in italics):

And as for that which He said, *That he who reads may read it speedily*, interpreted this concerns the Teacher of Righteousness, to whom God made known all the mysteries of the words of His servants the Prophets. *For there shall be yet another vision concerning the appointed time. It shall tell of the end and shall not lie.* Interpreted, this means that the final age shall be prolonged, and shall exceed all that the Prophets have said; for the mysteries of God are astounding.

The author of Psalm 37 is also thought to have had in mind the group which we call 'the Dead Sea sect' but which regarded itself as the chosen community of the last days. It is to emerge triumphant from the struggle against all evil powers, which will last forty years.

But those who wait for the Lord shall possess the land. Interpreted, this is the congregation of His elect who do His will. *A little while and the wicked shall be no more; I will look towards his place but he shall not be there.* Interpreted, this concerns all the wicked. At the end of the forty years they shall be blotted out and not an evil man shall be found on the earth.[15]

These Jews, too, read the ancient texts in the light of their own belief and experience, without any perceptible attention to what the biblical author had meant by his words in his time.

5. Jesus: man above scripture

We have seen that the canonization of the Torah was connected with attempts to strengthen the Jewish sense of community. We found a clear indication of this concern in the Letter of Aristeas:

Now our Lawgiver ... has fenced us round with impregnable ramparts and walls of iron, that we might not mingle at all with any of the other nations ...

24

In Jesus' version of Judaism, the divine book was not allowed to have this divisive role. He put the emphasis in quite another place. As the Jewish scholar Joseph Klausner remarked:

> His teaching became, on the one hand, the negation of everything that had vitalized Judaism; and, on the other hand, it brought Judaism to such an extreme that it became, in a sense, *non-Judaism*.[16]

The following sketch is an attempt to shed some light on this penetrating statement.

(a) His ministry

For years Jesus worked as a carpenter in the little town of Nazareth in Galilee. Nazareth, too, heard the sensational news that a prophet had arisen, a certain John, who was living in the hilly wilderness beside the River Jordan. To understand why this news caused such a stir at every level of the Jewish population, you must remember that people had been looking in vain for prophets for centuries. In 167 BC, pious Jews had uttered the lament of Psalm 74: 'We do not know what all this means for us: *there are no longer any prophets!*' The Greek ruler Antiochus was at that time engaged in making furious attempts to impose the Hellenistic way of life on the Jews in Palestine, the most southerly point of his immense kingdom. In December of that year he not only plundered the Temple in Jerusalem, 'the holy of holies', but even had sacrifices offered there to the idol which he had placed above the great altar of burnt offering. This abominable desecration was coupled with cruel persecutions in which thousands of Jews were killed because they refused to eat pork, circumcised their children, observed the sabbath laws and would not surrender their sacred books.

Three years after the desecration of the Temple the courageous Maccabees succeeded in defeating the military might of Antiochus. They removed all traces of pagan worship from the sadly battered Temple. But what were they to do with the altar of sacrifice? It had been desecrated by the abominable idol, but it was still a sacred object. The decision was made to dismantle it, says the well-informed author of I Maccabees, and 'they stored the stones in a convenient place on the Temple hill until there should come a prophet to tell what to do with them'.[17]

The lack of prophets was even more keenly felt, if that were possible, at the beginning of the Christian era. At that time the Romans ruled over Palestine. Herod and his sons had exploited the people. The leading priestly classes in Jerusalem tried to preserve their positions and possessions by various compromises with the occupying forces. Over against them stood the truly faithful Jews, united in the 'party' of the Pharisees. They did as much as they could to direct as many 'laymen' as possible to obey the Torah strictly, and thus to form an Israel worthy of the name, that is, a group which would be completely and utterly guided by the will of God as expressed in the Law. In this way it would be evident that he ruled over them, so that it was in fact possible to speak of a 'kingdom of God' on earth. But the Pharisees achieved this only with a relatively small group, a kind of religious upper class, because for the ordinary man the yoke of the Law was impossible to bear. He already had so many other burdens. He needed all his energy simply to get by. Moreover, there were many who wanted to have a real life, and that was not easy with the yoke of the Law on one's shoulders. So alongside the gulf between the worldly priests and the pious Pharisees, another, constantly deepening gulf opened up between those of God's people who saw themselves as 'the true Israel', who were faithful to the Law, and the great mass of ordinary people, dismissed by the pious with the old scornful term, 'the people of the land'. Even in this larger group, however, there were all kinds of tensions. In AD 6 the resistance movement had gone underground. In so doing, it had lost a few members, but it gained sympathizers time and again, whenever a harsh and hateful action by the Roman occupying forces caused nationalist feelings to flare up. Then in addition to the groups already mentioned there were others, like that of the Essenes, who in their own way were a 'true Israel', living out their exclusive holiness away from others.

What was to become of Israel, increasingly divided and torn apart? At the time when the Assyrians had swept over the land, God had called men like Amos and Isaiah and Micah to tell his people what the crisis meant. Later on, the prophets Jeremiah and Ezekiel were commentators on the Babylonian crisis. But for several centuries the time of the prophets had seemed past and gone. What now? To know God's intentions people had nothing but texts: the Torah and the other sacred books. They had texts, and those who studied them: scholars, and only scholars. These sifted out ancient prophecies and read books of Greek learning, and some wrote complicated 'apocalyptic' visions; all of it ivory-tower scholarship.

Hence the sensation when the rumour went around: 'A prophet has arisen, a genuine prophet!' If that were true, God had finally sent someone to proclaim to his people what he had in mind with this increasingly perilous crisis. Thousands went out to see and hear the man. He was dressed like Elijah of old, with an animal skin and a leather girdle. His message was as simple as it was demanding. The crisis which had come upon the Jewish community meant that God's judgment was at hand, and inevitable. No one could escape it. 'The axe is already laid to the root of the tree.' The only way to survive this terrible judgment was to begin a completely new life, 'to repent', as the ancient prophets had put it. Anyone who had made a firm decision to repent could demonstrate it by having himself immersed in the Jordan and coming out as a new man; this was a break with the whole of his sinful past.

It was quite an experience, in this musty muddle of text and interpretation, so suddenly to hear an authentic word from God demanding an answer in which one was so utterly involved. This involvement started with a ducking in the Jordan! Of course the orthodox Jews objected. Their doctrine was that only Gentiles and sinners would be affected by God's judgment and that the pious Jews, the true children of Abraham, would come through and live happily ever after. The retort of this tough new prophet was terse and forthright: 'It is no good your saying that you have Abraham as your father. I tell you that God can raise up children of Abraham from these very stones.' The Baptist's summons was addressed to everyone: when God comes in judgment, everyone will be held responsible for their actions, and no one will be able to claim a preferential place.

The carpenter from Nazareth also had himself baptized. But he did not return home. Apparently John had opened his eyes to his own task. It is probable that he first joined those who were helping the Baptist, but he soon went his own way.

Like John, Jesus proclaimed that God's judgment was at hand. He too called for 'repentance', but his preaching had a different character. He did not stay in the wilderness, but went to seek people out. With Jesus, the symbol of immersion, which John's converts had to choose for themselves, was replaced by the miraculous healing and liberation of those who gave credence to his words. He said a great deal, untiringly, about what concerned him. His teaching did not deal so much with the coming judgment as with the repentance that was required; he said what this must be and where it should lead. So it came about that Jesus was spoken of in two ways. On the one hand, he was seen as a prophet, like John, and thus as someone who did not interpret biblical texts but allowed God's word to be heard directly. On the other hand, because of his ongoing work of teaching, he was also addressed as 'rabbi', teacher. Yet he was different from the teachers to whom people were accustomed.

Jesus did not give the impression of being constantly preoccupied with the Torah and the other sacred texts. What emerges from the sayings of his that have come down to us is an intense interest in the people around him, and in their daily life and experience. Above all, the parables which are so characteristic of him reflect countless facets of the varied life of the houses, villages and towns in the Palestine of his day. Apparently he did not allow his attention to be monopolized by the study of scripture, but devoted it wholly and readily to all that he saw going on around him. He brought his experience spontaneously into his teaching. His comparisons are never strained. The ordinary experiences of ordinary people obviously said a great deal to him, and he saw them as pointing to the great values for which he stood.

All this has to do with the life of people in human communities. Jesus' interest in these relationships is also evident from his conduct. He liked to associate with all kinds of people. He was glad to be the guest of the well-to-do – indeed, he was fonder of this than might be thought to be becoming for a religious teacher. But he was equally at home with the poor and outcast, with those whom he might have been expected to avoid. These included the tax collectors, the 'publicans', who had bought from the Roman government the right to collect taxes. Men without too many scruples could become very rich in this way. To get their contracts, of course, they had to have friends among the occupying forces, and this was only possible if they were not too strict in observing the divine laws of purity and impurity, which forbade commerce with the heathen. So the publicans, the 'collaborators', were as abhorrent to the Pharisees as they were to the nationalists.

Jesus' association with them evoked severe criticism from the faithful. He answered them no less sharply: 'Those who are well have no need of a physician, but those who are sick.' He was aware that his friendship had a healing effect. A tax-collector in Jericho responded to his visit with the declaration, 'Behold, Lord, the half of my goods I give to the poor, and if I have defrauded anyone of anything, I restore it fourfold.'[18]

Jesus released unsuspected powers from the people whom he addressed, even from sick people who had turned to him in their despair. This despair was always in part religiously conditioned. Sickness was connected with sin and guilt. Consequently many sick people felt themselves excluded from the company of those who were in fellowship with God. Faith in Jesus seemed to have a redemptive and healing effect on them: 'Your faith has made you well.' Jesus also said, 'Your sins are forgiven you.' It is evident that a genuine encounter with him made possible a completely new start.

He asked some men from Galilee to help him in his proclamation. They entrusted their occupations and families to others and followed him. This shows how strong a persuasive power he exerted. Yet he never used compulsion. Often he simply appealed to the common sense and experience of his audience: 'If an ox that belongs to you falls into the ditch, you do not let it lie there . . .' One of his typical sayings was, 'Why do you yourself not judge what is right?' Sometimes he put a case to his audience and asked them what they thought about it. They were then compelled, not by him, but by their own insight, to conclude that he was right. The man who thought that he had fulfilled the two most important commandments of the Law, love of God and love of his neighbour, was still left with a problem. Who was his neighbour? Was it anybody at all? Jesus told him the story of the good Samaritan, someone who in the eyes of this faithful Jew was a reprehensible man, even more contemptible than the heathen. Then Jesus asked, 'Which of the three men who came along the road was a neighbour to the man who had been set on by robbers? What do *you* think?' The man whom Jesus addressed could hardly bring himself to say 'Samaritan', so he replied, 'The one who showed mercy to the unfortunate man.' Then this pious Jew had to be told that he must follow the Samaritan's example.

Sometimes Jesus himself was moved by the generosity which he evidently aroused. A man came to him who was willing to do anything to gain a share in eternal life, the blessing which Jesus promised. He had kept the great commandments from his youth upwards. What more could he do? Jesus looked at him in a very sympathetic way. The next thing to do, he said, is to sell all your possessions, give the proceeds to the poor, and follow me. This was asking too much. The man went away saddened. We are not told that Jesus then made an urgent appeal to his generosity, pursued him or threatened him. That was obviously not his way of doing things.

This approach is all the more striking because, as people said, Jesus spoke with so much 'authority'. He was quite different from the scribes. They presented texts from the Torah, and interpretations given by authoritative rabbis. Jesus seldom quoted scripture, and never used other peoples' interpretations. On the contrary, he declared on his own authority what God had really meant by certain commandments and prohibitions. He evidently felt quite at home with the God of Israel.

This was so evident that it was even noticed by non-Jews, like the Roman official in Capernaum. This man knew how to talk about authority. He himself had sworn an oath of loyalty to the divine emperor Tiberius. That was the basis of his own authority. One word from him could put a whole company of soldiers on the move. He detected something of the same sort in Jesus, something like an oath of allegiance, utter submission and dedication to his God. This had to be the source from which Jesus drew the authority with which he spoke and with which he gave commands to diseases and demons. Jesus had only to say one word, and the sickness would leave this officer's tormented servant.[19]

(b) What he wanted
What did Jesus have in view? What was his teaching? To what

did he summon people, so authoritatively and yet never with compulsion? We have seen that for him, as for John, God's judgment upon Israel was near. He too preached 'repentance'. But because, unlike the Baptist, he sought out people and associated with all kinds, he created many more possibilities of demonstrating how this repentance was to be shown. Consequently most of the sayings which have been handed down to us bear the mark of the circumstances, the situation in which Jesus found himself. They arise from meetings, questions from listeners, and criticisms from opponents. No summary of his 'doctrine' has come down to us, nothing that resembles a 'programme'. For that reason it is very difficult, if not impossible, to give a brief summary of what Jesus had in mind. What I shall say next can only be a small step in this direction.

Perhaps it could be said that Jesus strove for the formation of an Israel worthy of its name and its calling, an Israel that would be a true 'people of God'. In that case they would be a people of God as Jesus experienced him, and with whom he was very intimate. Jesus liked best to speak of this God as a father, the true Father of all men. 'Your father who knows what you have need of . . .' 'Your father who does not want one of these little ones to be lost . . .' 'Your father cares for the birds that neither sow nor reap nor gather into barns . . .' 'Your father who has numbered every hair of your head.' For Jesus, God was not the strict lawgiver and judge of every outward deed, as he had been for so many Jews since the Torah had been given such a central place. He was not the concentration of holiness concealed in the Temple, which one might not approach without taking the strictest precautions and which one might mention in conversation only with reverent paraphrases. Therefore Jesus conceived of that genuine people of God as a brotherhood, a family, consisting of children of a father whose sole concern and delight was to bestow gifts without discrimination, on the ungrateful and the evil as well as on the grateful and the good.

So what we might call Jesus' 'morality' or 'ethics' also refers exclusively to life together in community. Children of his God ought to be as generous as their Father, without being mean or discriminating. Giving only when they expect something in return can never be characteristic of them; according to Jesus, even 'the Gentiles' do that. When Jesus talks about 'the Gentiles', he is thinking of people who still have no idea of this Father, people who do not realize that all they are and all they have is a gift. Children of God know that they must live out his mercy and his forgiveness. That is why they must always be ready to forgive. 'How far should I go? Should I forgive my brother seven times?' To show Peter how silly it is to attempt to look for a standard here, Jesus takes things to extremes: 'No, I tell you, you must forgive seventy times seven!' [20]

A member of the family of this God was to accept his fellow man without reservation. Respect for the rights of others was included in belief in the God of Israel from the very beginning. The most fundamental of these rights was the right to live: 'You are not to kill.' Jesus demands a genuine respect for one's neighbour which goes a good deal further: we are not to allow even the first impulse to do away with someone to enter our hearts: 'I say to you that anyone who is angry with his brother has already made himelf guilty of his death.' Jesus goes to the root of human conduct. Even a desire for someone else's wife is to be condemned as adultery. A child of Jesus' Father must be utterly transparent, with no secret places in his heart. To be utterly transparent means to be at the mercy of others. According to Jesus, it is not right for the children of God to swear oaths. Their 'yes' or 'no' must be enough. They are not to bring in God on their side. Moreover, they are not to use good works to set themselves above others. It is good to pray and to fast, but prayer and fasting should be unobtrusive. People are to give generously to the poor, but they must not let others see what they are doing; they must even forget what they have done themselves. As Jesus put it, in his own inimitable way, 'Do not let your left hand know what your right hand is doing.' Take part in the kind of worship which is accepted in your community. But if you bring a gift to the altar and you feel that your brother has something against you, leave the gift and first be reconciled with your brother; then come back and offer your gift to God. For God is Father, and he can be honoured only out of a readiness to be reconciled with one's fellow men.

All this was in line with traditional Jewish morality. But it was carried further and made more radical. We might say that Jesus could not do otherwise, because God was so real to him. God was not an exalted, holy, supreme being, far removed from mankind; he took a fatherly interest in his creation, and especially in the crisis of the Jewish community and in the two men whom he had sent with this crisis in view, John the Baptist and Jesus.

At this point we might perhaps recall a prophet like Isaiah, in whom we can detect a similar association of ideas. An overwhelming experience of the God of Israel brings with it a keen awareness that a nation which, because of its unbelief, has parted from the Holy One, who desires to be known as the 'God of Israel', does not have much of a future. That is why Isaiah has no option but to proclaim a devastating judgment. For him, this is the real significance of the political crisis brought about by the Assyrian invasion. At the same time, however, this very awareness of God shows him how a renewed Israel can arise out of this 'judgment', a true people of God consisting wholly of 'believers'.

With due caution, we may perhaps try to understand Jesus in a similar way. If this is the right approach, we can see how he will have understood that the indescribable intimacy with God which he enjoyed was bound up with the crisis in which his people found themselves. In that case, in the light of such intimacy he saw more clearly than others how bad the situation was, and at the same time knew that he had been sent to give a last chance to that 'Israel', on the way to disaster as a result of violence from outside and division within.

This is also the reason why Jesus stated the moral demands of God so sharply. Now was not the time for quibbling over the commandments and prohibitions which had come down from the past, considering what one might or might not do. The situation, described in the Bible as 'the coming of God', called for radical repentance, a total commitment of the whole person. For a time, perhaps, Jesus may have hoped to bring all 'Israel' to repentance. He called some men to help him with his proclamation of God's coming. He deliberately limited the number of his followers to twelve, the ancient mark of the chosen people Israel which had twelve tribes. Thus this group was a living testimony to his intention to bring together the 'scattered sheep' to form a new people of God who would be worthy of the name Israel.

However, Jesus soon noted that his work was coming up against resistance. Criticism of what he was saying and doing from official leaders increased the more clearly he spoke out against them. Their objections made him put his message more and more clearly. In the end, they were forced to decide to eliminate Jesus.

Jesus was, in fact, causing trouble – a great deal of trouble. Ordinary people could be captivated by the warm and simple way in which he brought their God near to them. However, these people had no theological training. They did not detect that when he talked about God he described him in all too human terms. Moreover, Jesus offended in a much more serious way. As far as he was concerned, the Torah, the definitive and perfect revelation of God's will, was not the most important thing in the world. It was not that he denied the authority of the Torah, or attacked it directly. He did, however, believe himself to be empowered to interpret the Torah in his own way, and even to criticize some points in it. Sometimes he ignored even the most important commandments.

Take the law of the sabbath. The Book of Jubilees, which we have already come across, is one text which indicates the enormous reverence with which the sabbath was regarded at the time of Jesus. God himself was thought to join his angels in observing the sabbath in heaven. It was an exclusive prerogative of Israel to be allowed to join in the celebration. There was no clearer sign of Israel's election than the sabbath. Many Jews chose to let themselves be slaughtered rather than violate the sabbath law by taking up arms to defend themselves. Like all faithful Jews, Jesus took part in the synagogue service on this holy day. But if by doing so he could help anyone in distress, he did not hesitate to violate the prohibition against working on the sabbath, and simply declared: 'The sabbath was made for man, not man for the sabbath.'

This emphasis on 'man'[21] came first. Jesus committed the offence, indeed the heresy, of associating with Jews who felt themselves to be outside the Law. In this they had placed themselves outside the Jewish community, outside 'Israel', and as a result were in the same position as the mass of unclean heathen. When such people invited Jesus to meals, he accepted. He ate unclean foods, and by associating with people of this kind he must also have committed all sorts of other ritually unclean acts. On one occasion he justified his conduct by saying: 'There is nothing outside a man which by going into him can defile him; but the things which come out of a man are what

34

defile him.' In saying this he in fact declared that the law about clean and unclean foods was invalid. The real concern of this law was to bring home to the Jews an awareness of their separateness, whereas by contrast Jesus put forward a universal principle applying to all men. In that case, was he unaware of the countless faithful children of Israel who had suffered martyrdom rather than eat even a single piece of pork, from an unclean animal?

Many sayings have been handed down which show that Jesus often reacted very sharply to criticism from religious leaders. The story of the good Samaritan, which we have already mentioned, caused offence simply because Jesus showed how a man who was such an outcast from Israel could nevertheless teach the pious Jew a lesson. This in itself was galling. But in the story Jesus went even further. He told how the unfortunate traveller had been ignored by a priest and a Levite. This was in effect to say that the Jewish religious system was lacking in mercy. He made the point again and again, in a variety of circumstances. It is worth remembering the story of the scribes who bring to Jesus a woman taken in adultery. According to the Torah, this woman should have been stoned. What does Jesus make of her case? Is he to endorse the judgment of the Law? Or should he, for 'man's' sake, approve the sin and let this adulteress go her way? Jesus does not look up. He remains seated, bending forward and writing with his finger in the sand. Isn't he interested at all? Or does he feel repelled by these triumphant pietists who are prepared to end a human life in the name of their God? While they are waiting, he looks up and says: 'All right, of course the Law must be obeyed. But let the man among you who has not committed a sin cast the first stone.' Then he bends over and goes on writing in the sand. No one throws a stone. The official custodians of the Law leave one by one, beginning with the oldest. In the end, Jesus is left alone with the woman. Then at last he looks at her and says, 'Woman, where are they? Has no one condemned you?' She replies, 'No, no one.' Then Jesus says, 'Nor do I. Go, and do not be guilty of this wrong again.' There is no compulsion on anyone. The accusers have seen their guilt for themselves. The woman has been saved from her desperate situation. She has been given a new chance.[22]

Jesus had to be rendered harmless. He gave up his hope of bringing all 'Israel' to repentance. His vision of God's new people would indeed be realized, but through judgment, as a new life that God would raise up out of death. This death would consist in the destruction of the Jewish community, together with Jerusalem and the Temple. It would also consist in the destruction of Jesus himself. From the moment when he began to realize all this more clearly, he began to prepare the twelve, the nucleus of the new Israel, for such an eventuality. The morality which he had outlined was already a radical one. Never condemn your fellow man; that gives you very little to go on in your dealings with others. Love your enemies; that makes life a fearful adventure. It hands you over to others. Put an end to the escalation of evil by never hitting back, by responding to it with good; this makes you dependent on others. Forgive, again and again; this makes you defenceless. If you are to belong to the family of God which he is intent on gathering round himself, you must 'deny' your whole self. All this was radical enough. But now Jesus began to ask the twelve to go with him to Jerusalem. They could be certain of what would happen to him there. He was popular enough with the common people, at least in Galilee, to be hauled before the Romans as an agitator, a so-called 'Messiah', a leader of the national resistance movement. Every Jew knew that the Romans made short work of such figures. They always had crosses ready for them, which the rebels had to carry themselves to the place of execution. There had been hundreds of crosses on the roads leading out from the gates of Jerusalem. Now Jesus was asking the twelve to be ready to go with him, and as his followers even to be ready to carry their cross to the place of martyrdom. That was how far your devotion to God had to be able to go if you wanted to belong to the nucleus of the new Israel as Jesus saw it.

The new society was to consist of people who did not make too much of themselves. Its structure was to be quite different from that of accepted human societies. When some of the twelve indicated that they would like to play a leading part in the new people of God, they discovered that their desire could be satisfied. But in that case their leadership would have to consist in selfless service. No other ambition would fit in with this new community. Jesus made this clear at a meal with the twelve by taking upon himself a task which a slave would normally perform at a Jewish banquet. He washed their feet.

'Which is the greater, one who sits at table, or one who serves? Is it not the one who sits at table? But I am among you as one who serves.'[23]

At the trial of Jesus before the Sanhedrin, witnesses were brought who accused him of claiming that he would destroy the Temple in Jerusalem and build it again. This saying has been handed down to us in various forms. It probably goes back to one of Jesus' metaphorical remarks, in which he suggested that he would replace the Jewish religion of his time, the 'system' or the 'establishment', with a new form of society: the old 'Temple' would be replaced by a new one. This would explain why the word 'blasphemy' appears in the condemnation made by the Jewish judges. Jesus had laid hands on all that was holy to them, sanctified by an age-old tradition, hallowed by the blood of their martyrs, made sacred by the depth of their own daily commitment. That is why they had no choice but to remove him from their community once and for all.

6. Early Christian interpretation of the Bible

After his death, Jesus seemed able not only to bring together the scattered group of his closest followers, but to inspire them even more strongly than when he was travelling around with them. This inspiration also seemed to have an unprecedented power to attract others. First in Palestine, and soon afterwards in Syria, Asia Minor and Egypt, communities developed which were made up of people who had come together through their acceptance of Jesus as their Lord, and who allowed their way of thinking, hoping and living together to be determined by him. They believed that to some extent they were giving reality to the vision expressed in his preaching: a new family of God which was open to all people.

They saw all this as a 'fulfilment' of the old Israel. In its day, that old Israel had arisen, had been called together, made into a group, by a saving act of God. A common recognition of him, their deliverer, as the one and only Lord, made Israel what it was. But that Lord remained invisible; he spoke with his people through the mediation of Moses, and then through the prophets. Finally, the words given to them by God had been fixed in the sacred texts on the basis of which the Jewish community tried to find its own life. Now, in

Jesus, God had spoken much more directly than ever before. This man was no messenger from another. He had spoken on his own authority, and by accepting suffering and death he had completely identified himself with his message. To put it in his own words: he had 'gained his life by losing it'. By so totally losing it for the sake of others, he had gained life from God so abundantly that he could pass it on to all mankind without distinction. The new fellowship was not based on a written Law, a letter, but on the Lord who was alive and gave life through the Spirit.

Of course there was a great deal of talk and thought among the first Jesus communities about the amazing new experience of the members. At the outset, they had only the concepts and terminology of Judaism to develop and express the meaning of what had happened. But that was quite a lot. The Jewish community extended all over the then known world. We have already seen how its sacred books were translated into Greek, the common language of the greater part of the Roman empire. Of course that translation had contributed to the formation of an extensive Jewish-Greek vocabulary. The great Philo, whom we have already met, was only one of a number of Jewish thinkers. Even in Palestine before AD 70, there was a wide variety of Jewish life, with all kinds of groups and sects. There was also a great deal of reflection and discussion, mostly in Hebrew and Aramaic. We may assume that among the Jews of Palestine and elsewhere the level of intellectual development, as far as reading, writing, comprehension and powers of expression were concerned, was higher than in any other group in the civilized world of that time. It goes without saying that this was because of the primary role assigned to the sacred scriptures.

These scriptures were also regarded as sacred in the new communities which gathered around Jesus. The God who had expressed himself utterly in Jesus was, after all, the God who had sent Moses and the prophets and had inspired their writings. Because Jesus was the 'fulfilment', the climax of the age-old association between God and Israel, God had brought about all the earlier happenings and had arranged for them to be written down in a way which pointed forward to the climax. This gave rise to an entirely new interpretation of the sacred scriptures. As we have seen, Philo had read his philosophical insights and mystical experiences into them; rabbis had connected their innumerable rules of conduct with them; the Essenes saw the fate of their group, their founder and his enemies portrayed in them. In exactly the same way, the Christians now began to read the ancient scriptures in terms of their experiences and their faith. How Jesus had worked, what he had done and endured, his exaltation to the Father, his rule over the new people of God, for which he had laid the foundation – all this had already been described and foreshadowed by God in the scriptures. It had already been 'fore-told'. And in the same way, it was possible to discover from these scriptures what was going to happen next.

Out of all that was written and published in these first Christian communities, twenty-seven short writings have been collected together in what we call 'the New Testament'. They all bear witness to an intense and indefatigable preoccupation with the holy scriptures of the Jews. Seen in this light, the New Testament is modelled on the Jewish pattern; it is really a Jewish book. In a short chapter like this it is impossible even to begin to show the innumerable ways in which the scriptures are used in the New Testament. Every Christian who studied the Bible would use the definite methods of interpretation which had already been developed, combine them, or invent new ones based on them. Of course the ancient texts were also used in worship in a different way from their use in teaching and discussion, and Jewish Christians who were familiar with their Bible would use them in rather a different way from those who had a non-Jewish background. Because of this complicated situation, we can give only a few examples of the rich Christian interpretation of the Bible; the selection is an arbitary one, but it has been made with the modern reader of the Bible in mind.

(a) *Jesus the Messiah and the son of God*
We begin with two texts which many Jews saw as a description of the Messiah for whom they so longed. The word 'Messiah' means 'the anointed one'. This term was already applied in the stories of ancient Israel to the first king, Saul. David would not lift up his hand against Saul because he was 'the Lord's anointed'. David and his successors were also anointed ones of the Lord. After the collapse of the monarchy at the destruction of the kingdom of Judah in 587 BC, the ancient expectations of an end to history took on a 'messianic'

colouring. Many people thought that the major figure in this end to history, the Messiah, would be a king from the house of David who would make God's rule over the world clear once and for all, in the form of a perfect government, characterized by righteousness and peace. In Jesus' time, people looked for this Messiah as the one who would first of all deliver them from the intolerable yoke of the Roman forces of occupation, their Jewish collaborators, and all their other oppressors.

At a crucial moment in Jesus' dealings with the twelve he had asked them what they thought of him. Peter had said, 'You are the Messiah.'[24] Jesus did not reject the title, but said that they were not to use it in public. Too many people in a surge of gratitude wanted to foist on him the role of national liberator. In Jesus' eyes, Israel needed a much more radical liberation, from much more deeply rooted evils than the Roman occupation. And he already knew at that time that he would have to pay for his work of deliverance with his life. The religious leaders of the Jews could not do other than collaborate for this once with the priestly caste in Jerusalem, the Sadducees, and accuse Jesus to the Romans as the leader of a national liberation movement, a man who claimed to be the Messiah. Pilate was responsible for putting an inscription on Jesus' cross: 'the king of the Jews'.

After Easter, when the disciples felt the authority of Jesus even more strongly than when he was travelling around with them, it became abundantly clear to them that in Jesus God had fulfilled the ancient messianic expectations. Jesus was the one about whom David had spoken when he wrote in Psalm 110:

The Lord says to my lord, 'Sit at my right hand, till I make your enemies your footstool.'

This gave the disciples a way of expressing the new position, or status, of Jesus. He was now exalted by God, 'he sits at the right hand of God', and in this position he was addressed by David as 'my lord'. This explains the way in which the very first witnesses put it: Jesus of Nazareth, crucified by men, was now 'appointed by God to be Lord and Messiah'.

This had important implications. Psalm 2 also deals with the anointed one of the God of Israel. First God takes up the cause of his

Messiah. Then the Messiah himself speaks, and says that God has told him: 'You are my son; today I have begotten you.'

This psalm came from the court in Jerusalem. At that time people there had taken over much of the style and terminology which had found its way into Canaan from Egypt.[25] There are statues which the Pharaoh had placed at the right hand of the deity which was enthroned beside him. Often his feet rest on a footstool bearing a representation of his enemies, the enemies of his country. However, there are also reliefs in which the deity is handing on the principle of life to the mother of the Pharaoh: this is the way in which she 'receives' her child, for the ruling Pharaoh is the son of God. In the same way, the king of pre-Israelite Jerusalem was the son of the local deity. The Israelites took over the idea, but without thinking in such concrete terms. The new king was not begotten in this way through the queen mother. David was called from being a shepherd and anointed king. Time and again his successors became 'sons of God' on acceding to the throne. During the ceremonies they would keep hearing an oracle addressed to them: 'From this day forward you are my son, today I have begotten you.'

The prophet Nathan also put forward this idea in his famous promise to David. God would see to it that one of his sons would be his successor as king of Jerusalem, and of this man God said: 'I will be his father, and he shall be my son.'

Now the people of Israel as a whole was also called 'son of God'. An ancient account of the exodus from Egypt has Moses telling Pharaoh: 'Thus says the Lord, "Let my son go that he may serve me."' The prophet Hosea used the same imagery in his oracle: 'Out of Egypt I called my son,' a son who, according to Hosea, failed to appreciate his father. Disciples of the great prophet Isaiah used a stern accusation as a preface to their selection of his words:

> Sons have I reared and brought up,
> but they have rebelled against me . . .

Jeremiah, who was so sensitive to the way in which it was the nature of Israel's God to seek fellowhip, put his concern like this: 'I thought, you would call me My Father, and would not turn from following me . . .' So the people from Judah, when put to the test in the Babylonian exile, could learn to address God as Father: 'For you are our Father. For Abraham does not own us, and Israel does not acknowledge us; you yourself are our Father, our Redeemer is your ancient name . . . You are our Father; we the clay, you the potter . . . we are all the work of your hand . . .' This prayer was a response to the fact that from earliest times Israel had been called 'son'. A Jew found it quite impossible to attach any kind of physical significance to this term. He could think only of a relationship of mutual devotion. God had given his name to this people; they had to allow themselves to be guided only by his demands and his promises, and to belong only to him. In this way, they would exist among the nations as a reflection of God's personhood. The author of the book of Wisdom, who lived in Egypt shortly before the time of Jesus, pictures a pious Jew as being derided by his enemies like this: 'He claims to have knowledge of God, and calls himself a son of the Lord. He boasts of having God for his father . . . If the virtuous man is God's son, God will take his part and rescue him from the clutches of his enemies. Let us test him, with cruelty and with torture . . . let us condemn him to a shameful death, since he will be looked after – we have his word for it.'[26]

Thus Jesus' disciples were familiar with the phrase 'son of God' understood in some such terms; their master, however, gave it a distinctive character of his own. He stressed the aspect of mutual devotion, not least in being the reflection of God's personhood. In an unforgettable way, Jesus had addressed God with the familiar word 'Abba', the word a child uses to a parent. As members of God's new people, his followers had also to learn to use 'Abba' in their prayers. They could ask anything of God. 'Is there a man among you who would hand his son a stone when he asked for bread? Or would hand him a snake when he asked for a fish? If you then, who are evil, know how to give your children what is good, how much more will your Father in heaven give good things to those who ask him?' No listener could take exception to that 'who are evil men' on the lips of someone who so unreservedly took their part. It was a spontaneous expression of Jesus' feeling that in one particular respect he stood alone. This is also evident from his phrase, 'your Father'. He himself lived in a relationship with God in which he could not include others. This relationship was an integral part of the task to which he knew himself to be destined. He was prepared to burn himself up in seeking to fulfil it. To use his own phrase, he had come 'to light a fire on the earth', and he yearned for the time when it would blaze up. In this connection he himself would have to undergo some kind of baptism: 'How great is my distress till it is over.' This overwhelming consciousness of his mission set Jesus apart, even from his closest friends. For all his warm social contacts, at the deepest level he remained a solitary man. Sometimes misunderstandings and stupidity made him impatient: 'You faithless generation! How much longer must I be with you? How much longer must I put up with you?' In fact no one really understood him, or, to put it in biblical language, no one really 'knew' him. In a moment of elation he once spontaneously thanked his Father for his task of winning men to God. Perhaps this was the occasion on which he let it be known how he found the strength, in fearful human loneliness, to continue working: 'No one knows the son except the Father.'[27]

I mentioned earlier how Jesus produced a kind of mirror effect (the son resembles the Father). That is worth remembering in this context. When Jesus was attacked because he sought out tax collectors and sinners and shared meals with them, he told his accusers parables about the God who goes in search of the lost and rejoices greatly when he has found them.

(b) The scriptures in the gospels

Jesus gave his disciples sufficient hints for them to be able to recognize him after Easter as the long expected Messiah. They proclaimed him as Messiah and therefore also as 'son' of God. Now the sayings which I quoted earlier point to an intimacy which gave the term 'son' unprecedented significance. Jesus, the first Christians thought, must have belonged to God in a unique way, and must have come from him in the deepest conceivable sense. Indeed, he must already have been living with the Father before he began his career here on earth.

This idea, too, was in line with Jewish thinking. We saw earlier how people expressed the absolute authority of the Torah by saying that it existed with God before all other things. This idea had already been expressed earlier in terms of 'wisdom'. Perhaps at that time it had arisen out of a sense that Israel had developed its complex of regulations and rules for a happy life after the example of other, more ancient peoples. In one sense 'wisdom' was an international phenomenon, something 'universally human'. It was not one of the unique possessions of Israel, part of the complex of election and covenant, and therefore was antecedent to them. To put it in Israelite terms: wisdom was given to men at creation and therefore existed with God before creation. That is why, in the book of Proverbs, Wisdom could say: 'I, wisdom, who teach you all things for a happy life, was already born before the oceans were there . . . When God made the firmamant, I was already with him . . .'[28]

Consequently, Jesus' career did not begin with his baptism in the Jordan, nor his life with his birth. He had lived with God as an only son 'in the bosom of the Father'. Then God, having raised up so many men as prophets to speak his words to Israel, had finally sent his own son. Now the scriptures told an incomparable story about a man and his only son whom he loved. Abraham was ready to sacrifice his son Isaac. He was prepared to give up the most that could be asked of a man. Paul made use of the key words in that story when he wrote, 'If God is for us, who then can be against us? *He did not even spare his own son*, but gave him up for us all. And after such a gift will he not also give us all the rest?'

Although Jesus himself seldom used the word 'love', there was no better word with which to point to the heart of this divine enterprise. From the many terms available in Greek for expressing all kinds of attachment, the Greek-speaking church preferred to use the word *agape*, which was seldom found in everyday language. In this way the word was filled with a specifically Christian content. John even went so far as to use this term to point to the mystery that is God: 'Everyone who loves – practises *agape* – is a child of God and knows God. The man without this love does not know God, for God *is* love (*agape*). And the love which God is has been revealed among us by his sending his only son into the world in order to bring life.'

So in the eyes of his disciples, Jesus had a 'pre-history' in eternity. True, it was only after his death that he became their Lord in the most absolute sense of the word. On deeper reflection, however, it seemed to them that this 'post-history' had to be matched by a 'pre-history', a glory which Jesus possessed with the Father before the foundation of the world. As a result, they believed that his life had three phases. The middle phase was that of the humiliation: he had 'emptied' himself by assuming the form of a servant and becoming obedient even to death on the cross.

It is worth while remembering all this as you read the gospels. The writers say something about the ministry, the passion and the death of Jesus, this middle phase, but it is shot through with their belief in the pre- and post-history which they had discovered when they began to read the scriptures in the light of their overwhelming experiences with him.

Because Jesus 'fulfilled' the scriptures, those who told the story of his life found in the scriptures all sorts of material that more or less strongly influenced the form of their narratives. So even if it were possible to give a systematic account of the use of the Jewish scriptures in the gospels, we would need a thick book to tell the whole story. All I can do here is to give a couple of examples which may suggest just how the scriptures were used.

The most 'biblical' parts of the gospels are, of course, the stories connected with the birth of Jesus. As usually happens with figures of great historical importance, the beginning of Jesus' life only attracted attention many years after his death. It proved to be a point of reference for legends aimed at expressing the significance and the characteristics of his person. Jesus had come from Nazareth, and therefore had been known as Jesus of Nazareth or the Nazarene. As Messiah, however, he had to be a descendant of David, and he had to have been born in Bethlehem. That was what the prophet Micah had foretold. In Luke's account, Jesus' parents go to Bethlehem just before his birth, because of a census which the emperor Augustus is said to have decreed. Matthew's account simply has Jesus born in Bethlehem; at a later stage he moves on to Nazareth by divine instructions, because according to 'prophetic' texts (which Matthew does not clearly identify), he was 'to be called a Nazorean'.

Joseph was instructed to go to Galilee in a dream: the fourth time in the story that a revelation comes to him in such a way. His ancient namesake in the book of Genesis was also a man who received insights and instructions in dreams, and as a result was called 'the dreamer'. Both evangelists use a genealogy to show that Jesus was a descendant of David. This too was a necessary feature of the concept

45

of the Messiah; he could not be envisaged in any other way. It did not really matter how the genealogies were constructed: Matthew differs from Luke in the names he includes between David and Joseph.

The prophecy of Micah which identified Bethlehem as the birth-place of the future ruler over Israel went on to speak in enigmatic words about 'his origin in the days of eternity' and referred to his mother somewhat mysteriously as 'she who shall give birth'. Something of the same kind was to be found in the book of Isaiah. Ahaz, the unbelieving king, was given a sign: 'The woman is pregnant with a son who shall be called Immanuel, God with us.' The Greek translation had emphasized the mysterious character of the pregnancy by translating the word 'woman' as 'virgin'. This gave rise to the story that the mother of Jesus had conceived him directly, without having had intercourse with a man.[29]

Scripture offered a recognized term for such a divine intervention: the wind, storm-wind or breath of God; in Hebrew, God's *ruach*. In our Bibles, and in the language used in church, this word is always translated as God's 'spirit'. Such a rendering obscures the connection with blowing or breathing which was so obvious to men in biblical times. Blowing and breathing were mysterious phenomena to people of antiquity. A powerful wind can suddenly begin to blow without anyone being able to see it, which makes it an expressive symbol for God; and breath is an unmistakable sign of the mysterious life-force which is at work in both man and beast. Hence people were fond of talking about the wind or the breath of Israel's God (in our Bibles, God's 'spirit') at times when he had intervened 'stormily', or had stirred up men to excel themselves and become mighty deliverers of his people (his 'spirit' had made different men of them), or had caused his prophets to speak powerfully to them. After the exile, people also hoped that this *ruach* of God, the 'holy Spirit', would re-create those human hearts which were hardened in unbelief. After Easter, Jesus' disciples felt that they had become different people, and everyone who accepted this Jesus as Lord and consequently became members of the group which he gathered about himself, the new people of God, his 'church' or his 'body', were also aware that they had been given an entirely new start. All members of the community shared in this feeling. That too had been predicted by a prophet. According to Joel, at the consummation of history God would 'pour out his *ruach* upon all mankind, upon men and women, upon old and young, upon masters and servants . . .'[30] Now they were experiencing the fulfilment of these words. However, it seemed that this powerful new creative force had emanated from Jesus. It was in him that this powerful spirit had first been concentrated. Jesus himself had seldom spoken about the spirit of God. It had been the narrators who had introduced the spirit into the stories about him, as in the story of his baptism in the Jordan. And those who told of his virgin birth attributed his origin to the Holy Spirit.

In Luke's story, the birth of Jesus is first announced to shepherds. Whereas most of the details of his sensitive chapters about the beginning of Jesus' life have been borrowed from the scriptures and are modelled on Old Testament narratives, the shepherds seem to have been inspired by what Luke most admired in Jesus' conduct: his preference for the despised and the outcast. He evidently knew that the middle-class society of Jerusalem had no time for shepherds, those unclean people from the wilderness, so impudent and untrustworthy that they could only be called 'sinners'. That is why Luke arranges that the good news of the Messiah shall be first announced to them. Matthew, too, allows his account to be influenced by a later situation. In his congregation, people were constantly amazed at the fact that the leaders of the Jewish community had rejected Jesus, whereas increasing numbers of non-Jews accepted him as the Lord to whom they gave the best of themselves. As a result, Matthew tells how Gentiles come from the East, having had their attention drawn by a star (as happens in several Jewish stories) to the birth of the Messiah. The biblical texts are full of the wisdom of the East. That was where astronomy came from. Yet with all their learning, these men still did not know where to look for the new-born Messiah. Only the Jews themselves knew that, because they possessed the scriptures, the prophecies. The chief priests and scribes also passed on the information they had been given: the Messiah would be born in Bethlehem. They themselves, however, did not go to worship him. The wise men from the Gentiles did this, bringing him the gifts which had already been presented in the scriptures, in Psalm 72 and Isaiah 60. In the latter text the gifts were

47

in fact brought by the Gentiles to 'Zion'; Zion was a symbol for the chosen people who are once again accepted by God in grace, and who represent, 'reflect' him on earth. However, the Messiah does this in a much more intense and definitive way.

This theme recurs in the sequel to Matthew's account. The destiny of Israel is as it were recapitulated in Jesus' career. That is why Matthew makes Jesus' parents flee with their child to Egypt. Joseph is commanded to do this in a dream. As a result, he can realize the saying of Hosea's that we have come across already: 'Out of Egypt I have called my son.'

However, as leader of the new people of God, Jesus also 'fulfils' the figure of Moses. The book of Exodus begins by telling how divine providence saved the baby Moses from a massacre of Israelite children. For Matthew, king Herod plays the role of the murderer. He can connect this with Jeremiah's remark about Rachel weeping for her children, because in his time Rachel's tomb was thought to be in the region of Bethlehem.

In biblical thought, the concept of 'servant' is very closely related to that of 'son'. The life of the devoted servant is wholly determined by the commands and the wishes of his master. It is possible as it were to infer the personality of the master from the doings of his faithful servant. Israel was marked out by the fact that she served this one God and recognized no other power, or at any rate was not allowed to recognize any other power. All kinds of individual 'servants' appeared to spur Israel on to the exclusive service of her God. The lives of Moses and of so many prophets after him were wholly determined by their task of securing Israel's utter commitment to the service of this God. An anonymous servant appears in many passages in the second part of the book of Isaiah: he is utterly devoted to God, and God is utterly devoted to him. Sometimes he seems to be a personification of Israel; more often he is clearly an individual who has a task to fulfil for that nation, a task which has an effect on other nations. In his person he seems to be the embodiment of the devotion and the submissiveness of Moses and Jeremiah and the other prophets. This 'ideal' servant continues to fulfil his task of winning over rebellious Israel to the very end. To the astonishment of the other nations, he is slain as a sin offering for the sins of all, and as a consequence God bestows on him abundance of life. Thus he can make unnumbered multitudes righteous; in other words, he can bring them into living communion with his God.

We cannot know for certain whether Jesus himself thought of his task in the light of Isaiah's ideal servant. However, the whole of the New Testament shows that his disciples took such a line, in a variety of ways. In this connection we should remember that many Jesus groups emerged rapidly in Greek-speaking settings, where people used the Greek translation of the Jewish scriptures. And in Greek, *pais* could mean both 'servant' and 'son'.

In the story of Jesus' baptism in the Jordan, a voice from heaven seems to combine two biblical texts: the words addressed to the Messiah in Psalm 2, 'You are my son', and those in Isaiah 42 with which God introduces his servant: 'Behold my servant in whom I am well pleased.' We have already seen how it was John's summons which drew Jesus from Nazareth. Perhaps it was at his baptism that he had a first glimpse of his future task. Be this as it may, his disciples later regarded his baptism as the decisive moment, the moment of his 'call'. However, Jesus' call was not like that of the prophets, who only received their function and their credentials as prophets at the moment of their call. For in Jesus' case, the author has the voice from heaven (or the 'inspired' words from scripture) confirming who Jesus already *is*. It is true that the descent of the spirit in the form of a dove points to the conviction that this was the time when Jesus embarked on his life-giving activity.

In the sequel, Jesus remains in the wilderness for forty days, just as Israel remained in the wilderness for forty years after passing through the waters of the Red Sea. Like Israel, in this situation Jesus was put to the test. This theme clearly played a part in the formation of the story; one need only read Deuteronomy 8 alongside it to see how this can be so. However, the story shows Jesus face to face with Satan, the great adversary of God and men. Satan puts forward suggestions which coincide with the temptations to which Jesus was exposed during his ministry: concern for himself, success through spectacular miracles, and the desire for power. It may be that his disciples collected them and combined them at a later stage to form this introduction. Possibly too we have here a symbolic indication from Jesus himself, explaining how after his baptism he had

49

'bound the strong man' by setting his own steadfast determination against other possibilities which were there to entice him.

Some of the miracle stories in the gospels are shot through with themes from the Jewish scriptures.[31] Jesus is always 'the fulfilment' of them. For example, the scriptures told how Moses had fed his people in the wilderness with miraculous food, manna. They also told how the prophet Elisha had fed a hundred men with a couple of loaves of bread, providing such a banquet that there was something left over. A story went the rounds in the Jesus communities about the feeding of several thousand people who had followed Jesus into the wilderness; this was an evident 'fulfilment'. The evangelist Mark already knew at least two versions of this story which he incorporated into his book. In both cases, the way in which Jesus takes the bread, blesses it and distributes it is reminiscent of his action at the last supper, which was being performed by Christians weekly. The repeated experience of this miraculous feeding also had an influence on the form of the story.

On more than one occasion Jesus had referred to the figure of Jonah and to the inhabitants of Nineveh, who had been converted by his preaching. The short story about Jonah's adventures was well-known. It had probably influenced the story of how Jesus stilled a storm. In the story, Jonah was trying to escape the task he had been assigned, and took a boat bound for Tarshish, in exactly the opposite direction from Nineveh. Such a severe storm arose that the ship was in danger of sinking. Jonah, however, was unaware of this; he was fast asleep. In the same way, Jesus slept peacefully in the stern of a boat which was about to sink, along with all his disciples, in a sudden violent storm. But Jesus was a 'fulfilment' of Jonah, in the sense that he was obedient to God and therefore had sovereign control over diseases and demons and all the forces of nature. For those who first told the story, the boat was a figure of the church, which when danger threatened joined the biblical believers in praying, 'Awaken, O Lord!'

Many themes from the Bible can be seen in the story of the 'transfiguration'. This takes place on a high mountain, which is left unnamed. Indeed it could not be named, because it was not a mountain in Palestine. It was the 'mount of God' on which the great revelations took place: there Moses and Elijah were permitted to see something of the divine glory. Jesus' face suddenly became radiant, and his garments became luminous. He was dazzling, like the heavenly figures who appear in some books of the Bible, for example in Daniel 10. Then the two men whom people expected to see on the mount of God appeared: Moses and Elijah, i.e. the Law and the Prophets. Jesus began to talk with them. These two groups of books contained the prophecies that the Messiah had to suffer in order to be able to enter into his glory. Luke, who emphasizes this point so strongly, explains the story by saying that Jesus' conversation with them was about 'his exodus which he would accomplish in Jerusalem'. Then the cloud, the traditional biblical symbol of the presence of God, appeared. A voice from the cloud uttered the very biblical texts which were pronounced at Jesus' baptism in the Jordan, and then added a saying of Moses. In Deuteronomy 18, Moses prophesies that God will raise up a prophet after him, and then he commands: 'You must listen to him.'

Finally, there are the stories about Jesus' passion and death. Here texts and themes from the scriptures were soon introduced into the reminiscences of eye-witnesses. Some of the psalms are the utterances of a believer who prays in the hour of his deepest need: illness, attacks, enemies all threaten his life. Then suddenly his prayer turns into a song of praise to the God who has heard his prayer and has rescued him from the clutches of the 'underworld'. He begins to give a thank-offering, *eucharistia*, for the new life which God has given him, and he invites all those who truly seek after God to join him in it. In psalms of this kind, 'David' was obviously not speaking in his own name, but was prophesying the fate of his distant descendant, the Messiah, just as Isaiah had done in his oracles about the ideal servant of the Lord.

The author of the prayer in Psalm 22, 'My God, my God, why have you forsaken me?', describes how his enemies ridicule his trust in the help of Yahweh. Moreover, 'they divide my garments among them, and cast lots for my raiment'.

The author of Psalm 69 has become a stranger to his brethren because 'zeal for your house, O God, has consumed me'. His enemies have given him poisonous food and 'in my thirst they gave me vinegar to drink'.

In Zechariah 9–14 the Christians found a mysterious prophecy of

51

what would happen in the days of the consummation. The passage began with a summons to Jerusalem to welcome her king with rejoicing. He would come 'righteous and triumphant, humble and riding on an ass, and proclaiming peace to all the nations of the earth'. Later on there is mention of 'a flock without a shepherd'. This theme then leads on to the image of a shepherd who receives his wages in the form of 'thirty pieces of silver'; at God's command he then throws the money, the usual price for a slave, 'before the potter in the Temple'. The prophecy goes on to deal with the inhabitants of Jerusalem who 'shall look on him whom they have pierced', and about whom they raise a lament 'as over an only son'. Before long the theme of the shepherd returns; the shepherd is smitten, 'so that the sheep are scattered'. The closing sentence of Zechariah's obscure prophecy consists in the prediction that 'on that day there shall no longer be any trader in the Temple of Israel's God'.

This last point was clearly fulfilled by Jesus when he drove the money-changers and the merchants out of the Temple, and he made the earlier part of the prophecy come true when he rode into Jerusalem on an ass. Thus there was every reason to use other details of Zechariah's prophecy in the accounts of these crucial events.

Their climax was the death of Jesus. It brought to an end the whole of previous history and opened up the new, final, definitive era. Before long people were relating how at that very moment the veil of the Temple was rent from top to bottom. This was a significant symbol: God was now no longer concealed and inaccessible; the old Temple had served its purpose. Very soon people also began to talk of impressive natural phenomena. Luke mentions an eclipse, Matthew an earthquake so powerful that it splits the rocks. These phenomena are also derived from the scriptures. Many ancient biblical texts represent nature as reacting to an intervention on the part of the God of Israel. This will also happen in the end, on the great day. Thus Amos prophesied:

> And on that day I will make the sun go down at noon,
> and darken the earth in broad daylight.[32]

Perhaps the attention of Christians was drawn to this text because immediately after it Amos talks of 'mourning for an only son'.

Even from these few scattered examples we can understand something of the nature of the four gospels. They preserve reminiscences of Jesus' person and conduct, but these are set in a biblical frame, a biblical context. Perhaps a better comparison would be with a tapestry: recollections of what Jesus did, said and suffered were intertwined, sometimes inextricably, with what *had to have* happened because Jesus was 'fulfilling' the ancient scriptures. To put it in another way: people were describing *at one and the same time* the mysterious and attractive person with whom they had been in contact and the Son of God who he proved to be in the light of the Easter experiences, the Messiah who was announced and described in so many of the biblical texts.

(c) The scriptures in the letters of the apostles

We began with the use of the Old Testament in the gospels, because they are what people are most familiar with. We do, however, have still earlier evidence of that use of the scriptures, in the letters of Paul. It is worth while considering a few instances of the way in which he used these ancient scriptures in thinking through, defending and formulating his new faith.

Paul had received his religious education at the feet of the famous rabbi Gamaliel. He stood out above his fellow-pupils in his zeal for the Torah and the traditions of his ancestors. Thus he became familiar with the many ways in which Pharisaic insights and life-style, their views of God and man, of salvation and damnation, were based on the scriptures. That was why Paul fought so vigorously against those who worshipped the crucified Jesus of Nazareth as Messiah. Paul had learnt enough about him to see that he had been the opposite of a Messiah. He had undermined the principles of the Jewish community. One could see this clearly from his pack of followers: almost all of them were people who did not live in accordance with the Law – they were 'fringe church people'. Were these to be the chosen people of the Messiah? Even worse, this heresy was spreading like an epidemic. Jewish communities outside Palestine were already being infected with it.

Paul's battle against this heretical movement was radical enough; once he had been struck by the new view of Jesus as though by a bolt of lightning, his commitment to that was equally vigorous.

More clearly than many of the earliest disciples, he immediately saw the dimensions of the new people of God which Jesus had in view. Jesus had included all those who could not bear the yoke of the Law, all those who were officially excluded from salvation. But in that case this great mass of the excommunicated, those whom the Jews called the nations, *goyim*, 'heathen', would also have to be included in the people of God.

Because he had been crucified, according to the Law Jesus was accursed: 'Cursed be he who hangs on a tree.' Now if God had appointed him Messiah, then God had invalidated his own Law. In that case, all those who were accursed according to the Law could be incorporated into the people of this Messiah.

Years later, looking back at the change of fortunes in his life, and thinking of his youthful zeal for the Law and of the way in which he had persecuted the Christians, Paul wrote: 'But then God, who had set me apart before I was born, called me by his grace, was pleased to reveal his Son to me, in order that I should preach him among the Gentiles.' He had received that new vision of Jesus as a commission. It is certainly no coincidence that he begins the sentence I have just quoted with words spoken by the servant of God in Isaiah 49:

> You coastlands, listen to me;
> Listen attentively, you distant peoples:
> The Lord has called me from the moment of my birth . . .[33]

Paul could not help thinking of this totally new thing that had come to him in terms of the scriptures that he knew. Thus he formulated his task in the words of the servant in Isaiah, who was destined to take God's salvation to the ends of the earth.

At the same time, Paul also discovered the universalistic note in all kinds of other biblical texts. Thus in various psalms David had spoken about the Gentiles who would come to praise God, and sometimes he summoned them explicitly to this task. Its fulfilment was now in process, and Paul had been given the privilege of sharing in the work.

However, it still remained difficult for many Jews who accepted Jesus as Messiah to follow Paul. It was difficult for them to grasp that Gentiles could be incorporated into the people of the Messiah without any formalities. Generation after generation it had been

54

impressed on them that circumcision was a necessary condition of belonging to the chosen people, that it was essential to abstain from unclean foods, in short, to fulfil the major commandments of the Law. It was necessary to do something to share in the salvation of the Messiah. Was not Paul making membership all too easy?

In his discussions with these Christians Paul always used his Bible, which he read with them in the Greek translation. The passages in his letters where he examines various details of the story of Abraham are the best-known illustration of these discussions.

In chapter 17, the book of Genesis describes how God commanded Abraham to circumcise himself and all his male descendants: this was the sign of their special bond with God, the token of their 'election'. But Paul points out that even earlier in the story in Genesis, in chapter 15, God had made this covenant with Abraham, and Abraham had trusted in his promise of offspring.[34] This faith made Abraham righteous in God's eyes. So we read in the book of Genesis. Now, Paul points out, Abraham was not circumcised at that time. While yet uncircumcised, therefore, he could become the 'father' of the Gentiles who were now entering the people of God, as he could become 'father' of Jews who took the step in the same faith and did not appeal to the privilege of their circumcision. In this way, Abraham could become the father of many nations.

Paul goes still further. Abraham's faith was not essentially different from that of the Christians. For the story in Genesis says that Abraham was a hundred years old when a son was promised to him, at a time when the womb of his aged wife Sarah had long since been 'dead'. Yet he trusted that God would fulfil this promise. It was therefore a matter of complete trust in the one who awakens life out of death. Well, Paul pointed out, that is precisely the nucleus of the new faith: utter trust in the God who has raised the crucified Jesus to life and has made him the central figure of the new people of God who participate in his new life with God. A better way of putting it might be to say that they participate in the new family of God. For Paul follows the example of Jesus in saying that all people have a share in 'the sonship' which belongs to Christ by nature. That implies many things. After all, a son inherits his father's possessions; thus through their faith Christians are 'fellow-heirs'.[35]

Sometimes Paul's use of biblical texts reminds us of Philo. The

Greek text of Genesis says that the promise was given to Abraham 'and his seed'. Paul points out that the form here is not plural 'and to his seeds', but singular. So the text refers to Christ. To us this interpretation seems rather artificial, all the more so because Paul was familiar with the Hebrew text and knew that the word for 'seed' used here has a collective significance, meaning 'posterity, progeny'. But this interpretation, or rather reading in, is placed entirely at the service of his train of thought, which in fact makes a good deal of sense. For here he sees the promise to Abraham as a kind of divine testament. Now according to the Greek text of the book of Exodus, the Law came four hundred and thirty years after that testament. It could not annul the promise that had been made, and therefore it had another function, which necessarily ceased when the promise was fulfilled in the 'seed', Christ, the heir.

Anyone who knows how to read the Law properly can see pointers to the new salvation everywhere, even the situations in which it is now being realized. Paul can understand how Jews remain bound to the Law; they consider themselves under an obligation to be circumcised and to observe all the other usages which put up barriers between them and others; their customs are in fact aimed at hindering communication with others. Moreover, they annoy Christians, because Christians regard all practices which lead to isolation and disrupt communication as outmoded and superfluous. There are also indications of this situation in the scriptures. There too we find an unfree figure who presents problems to a free one. We are told how Abraham fathered a son, Ishmael, by his slave girl, Hagar. When this son annoyed his half-brother Isaac, he was sent into the desert with his mother. Ishmael, the son of the slave woman, was not to share with Isaac in Abraham's inheritance. Isaac was the son whom God had given, in faithfulness to his promise, to Sarah, the free woman. In passing, Paul points out that Ishmael (the ancestor of the Arabs) was sent into the Arabian desert; it is no coincidence that this is the location of Sinai, the mountain on which the Law was given. Present-day Jews, the slaves of the Law, are represented by this Hagar, the slave girl, and mother of a slave. We Christians are Isaac, children of the promise, who belong to another Jerusalem, so different from the earthly city which is the focal point of Jewish servitude.[36]

56

'You shall not muzzle an ox when it is treading out the grain.' So the Law commands. For us modern men this is testimony to the spirit of the book of Deuteronomy, which here, as elsewhere, prescribes humane treatment for animals. But for Paul, and for all Jewish and Christian readers in antiquity, this was a word of God, communicated through Moses to his people. Paul finds it hard to believe that at this point God is simply concerned with animals. Of course he is concerned with human beings, and in the light of Christ this passage must refer to the new situation. For everything must have been written 'for the sake of those of us who are experiencing the fulfilment of the ages'. The meaning of this word of God must therefore be that the person who devotes all his time to providing spiritual food for Christians has a right to require from them support for his physical needs.

These are only some examples of the very varied use of the Jewish Bible which can be found in Paul's own letters. The use in the other writings of the New Testament is even more varied. It is extraordinarily elaborate in the letter to the Hebrews, a profound message of encouragement to Christians with a Jewish background, who have to suffer at the hands of their former companions, and who are so discouraged that they feel homesick for the majestic ceremonies in the Temple of Jerusalem of which they were so fond. The author of this document, which is written in excellent Greek, must have reflected for many years on the ancient scriptures in the light of the new faith. With great skill he uses all the traditional Jewish methods of interpretation to show how in Christ, the Son of God and the true High Priest, Israel's ancient worship has been completely 'fulfilled'.

One example of biblical interpretation in the Letter of James is of interest in connection with our theme. The author regards mere faith, without 'works', as a very dangerous thing. It is all very well believing that there is one God, but so do the devils. 'Do you want to be shown ... that faith apart from works is barren? Was not Abraham our father justified by works, when he offered his son Isaac upon the altar? You see that his faith was active along with his works, and faith was completed by works.'[37] In this way the scripture was fulfilled which says, 'Abraham believed, and it was reckoned to him for righteousness.' At first glance this appears to be polemic against Paul; both of them use the same biblical texts.

In the same connection James also cites the case of Rahab the harlot. According to the book of Joshua she was justified on the basis of her works; she had hidden the spies in her house and had helped them to escape from Jericho. Later on we shall meet Rahab again, because of her Christian career, of which James marks the beginning.

7. The new Bible and the church fathers

The biblical terms 'spirit' and 'spiritual' are very difficult to define, and therefore they give rise to a good deal of misunderstanding. We have already come across the Hebrew word *ruach* and the Greek word *pneuma*. To the people of the Bible these words meant wind and breath, or the stormy events in which they detected the dynamic presence of God.

To our mind, the word 'spiritual' always evokes the idea of something non-material, incorporeal, whether or not it has such connotations as 'higher' or 'inward': a person's inner life is hidden, in contrast to his outward conduct. But this is not what the people of the Bible meant. When Luke sums up the spiritual experiences of the first disciples in an event which he locates at Pentecost, he introduces characteristically biblical images: 'a rushing sound as of a mighty wind' and 'tongues as of flame' which cause the disciples to burst out into enthusiastic testimony. In addition, Luke notes the kind of impression that the spiritual experience of the Christians made on outsiders: 'These men are drunk.'

So the working of the Spirit is spectacular. However, that does not mean that it is any the less inward. We must even say that the working of the Spirit becomes visible because it has penetrated to the deepest level of the human heart. This Spirit has destroyed the last bulwarks behind which selfishness still tries to shelter. It has opened up mankind, and rescued men from their state of isolation. Man has become open to all others. Like Jesus, people can address God as 'Abba', and welcome their fellow men as brothers. The bond that unites him to them is intense, because it has very deep roots. That is why the group can be called 'the temple of the Holy Spirit', as well as 'the body of Christ'.

When the Christians of this earliest period talk about reading the Jewish Bible in a spiritual way, they are talking about relating the ancient text to their present experience in this new community of which Jesus is the living centre. We have come across a couple of examples of this new, 'spiritual' interpretation in the previous chapter. They did not include a well-known passage from Paul's Second Letter to the Corinthians. Paul points out that the Jews cannot understand the real meaning of their holy scriptures because they refuse to recognize Jesus as Messiah. First Paul writes like a rabbi (which makes him rather difficult for us to understand), talking about the veil which (according to Ex. 46) Moses had to put over his face. Then he goes on:

> Their minds were hardened; for to this day, when they read the old covenant, that same veil remains unlifted, because only through Christ is it taken away. Yes, to this day whenever Moses is read a veil lies over their minds; but when a man turns to the Lord the veil is removed. Now the Lord is the Spirit, and where the Spirit of the Lord is, there is freedom.[38]

Here Paul is talking about things which were constantly in his thoughts and which had become a regular preoccupation. They included the utterly new experience which had come to him and to his fellow Christians, along with the other side of the coin, which was a constant problem to him. How was it possible that so many Jews could miss this new experience? They remained closed to the real, 'definitive' meaning of the scriptures which God had disclosed to them.

For Christians, the traditional Bible had in fact become a new book by virtue of the 'spiritual' interpretation through which it was understood. In later centuries, however, there was yet another reason for talking about a new Bible. By virtue of a process which is difficult for us to trace in detail, a number of writings from first-century Christianity attained the same status as the Jewish Bible. They were thought to be inspired in just the same way. So there came into being the collection that was soon to be called *the* Bible, *the* book *par excellence*. (Bible comes from the Greek *biblos*, 'book', the diminutive of which is *biblion*, and the Latin *biblia*.)

The twenty-seven writings which were added to the Jewish sacred books were called 'the New Testament', but Christians felt that they formed an organic whole with what they began to call the Old

Testament. This came about first of all because the New Testament books bore witness to salvation in Christ in images and terms which almost without exception were borrowed from the Jewish writings. But it also came about because the new writings, too, were interpreted spiritually. For the new reality which Christians were experiencing on the one hand was a 'fulfilment' of what had happened and what had been written before Christ, and on the other was still open to further fulfilment. Paul had already pointed this out in his inimitable way, in words which Christians are never likely to forget: 'We know (God's secrets) in part.' For the moment, we see the ultimate things which God has prepared for those who love him only 'as in a mirror, dimly', in comparison with the perfect fellowship in Christ which God will eventually grant us when we shall see him 'face to face'.[39] So the common life of Christians here and now is childlike, immature. Even our most sublime utterances are no more than childish stammering. Whatever we attempt to express about salvation is always only a pointer towards reality. This is the case even with what we find in the New Testament, and in its most prominent books, the gospels. What Christ says and does and suffers there has a dimension which escapes the superficial, 'non-spiritual' reader. For him it is nothing but an account of events which belong irrevocably to the past. Only the person who relates them to what he is experiencing now, as a member of the church on the way to fulfilment, in other words, only someone who reads them 'spiritually', will understand what God is trying to say to him here and now through the texts.

To make this more specific, and less remote for modern readers, I am going to give some examples of the way in which the church fathers interpreted the Bible. I shall begin with Origen, who had more influence on the Christian interpretation of the Bible than any other church father.

Origen was born about the year 185 and was given his first schooling in Alexandria by his father Leonidas. Shortly after 200, Leonidas was martyred for his Christian beliefs. After some years of university studies, Origen was made responsible by the bishop of Alexandria for instructing the catechumens there, the new converts to the faith. In due course Origen delegated this task to his pupil Heracles, which enabled him to devote more time to his studies, and to travels in furtherance of them which took him to Palestine and Arabia and even to Rome. Because of difficulties in Alexandria, in about 230 he moved to Caesarea on the coast of Palestine, which at that time was a flourishing centre of Christian life. There too he devoted himself unsparingly to the study of Christianity, on the basis of an indefatigable preoccupation with the Bible, from which he preached almost every day for many years.

This much travelled theologian knew almost all there was to be known at the time about Christianity and its relationship with Judaism and the pagan world. This wealth of experience, distilled through Origen's own perceptive and thoughtful mind, came to be expressed in his innumerable writings. Unfortunately, however, many of them have been lost. For Origen was compelled to be original on all sorts of points of Christian thought. He was called upon to give answers to questions which had never been raised before, and to which no carefully thought out and recognized answers were available. So it came about that in the following centuries he became the subject of heated theological disputes. As a result, many of his writings were so to speak taken out of circulation and ceased to be copied. It is fortunate that a number of his interpretations of the Bible were translated into Latin as early as the fourth century. They were held in great esteem in the western church, so people continued to copy the texts there down the centuries and his influence on Latin Christianity was decisive. One scholar has commented, 'To write a history of Origenist influence on the west would be tantamount to writing a history of western exegesis.'[40] Here is Origen's sermon on Exodus 2: Pharaoh's daughter has found a child in a basket; she has him brought up, welcomes him into her palace and gives him the name Moses:

Every word of this text contains a boundless mystery. It would require a great deal of time to expound this, and if we wished to draw out everything that is in it, an entire day would not be sufficient. But let us try to say something about it briefly, for the edification of the church. I think that one can see in Pharaoh's daughter the image of the church, which is assembled out of the heathen nations. Although her father is evil and godless, it is said to her from the mouth of the prophet: 'Listen, my daugher, consider and incline your ear: forget your people and your father's house, for the king is captivated by your beauty.' Thus she leaves the house of her father and goes to the water in order to wash away the sins which she has committed in her paternal home. Then she is immediately moved by feelings of compassion and takes pity on the child. Thus this church which comes from the heathen finds Moses in the swamp. Moses who is rejected by his own people and left as a foundling. She has him brought up among his own people, where he spends his childhood. But when he is grown, he is brought to her and then she takes him to be her son. We have already often explained that Moses signifies the Law. Thus also the church, when she comes to the waters of baptism, receives the Law which lay hidden there in a basket that was covered with pitch and tar. The Law was enclosed in a wrapping like that; it was covered with pitch and tar, entangled in the cheap and earthly interpretations of the Jews, until the church of the nations came to take her out of the muck and mire of the swamps and to give her a place in the royal courts and palaces of Wisdom. Nevertheless the Law spent her childhood in her own people. It is true that among those who are incapable of understanding her spiritually she is very small, a child that is fed with milk that is for children. But when she comes to the church and enters into that house, she becomes a Moses who is strong and robust. When one has once thrown away the veil which is the letter, then one finds in the reading of the law a food that is substantial and perfect.

In this illuminating text, it is worth noting how the figures of Moses and of the Law which he wrote are intertwined. Origen shared in the great veneration for the figure of Moses which was and is so characteristic of Jewish tradition, particularly in Alexandria, where Philo had lived. For Origen too, Moses was the most highly favoured of all the favoured figures of the Old Testament. David and Isaiah may have been vouchsafed a very clear vision of the incarnate son of God whom they foretold, but Moses had a more intimate association with God than any other man, and fully comprehended the deepest spiritual meaning of the laws and stories which he wrote down. The light that was to become manifest in Christ was given in advance to him and all these others. They borrowed their brilliance from him; the actual meaning of their writings becomes clear only in his light. That is why the story of the transfiguration of Jesus on the mountain appears so often in Origen's discussions and sermons. At one point he writes:

If anyone has seen and beheld the Son of God when his visage is altered so that his appearance is like the sun and his clothing like the light, then Moses (that is, the Law) suddenly appears to him, and in Moses' company Elijah as well; not these alone, but there also appear to him all the prophets in conversation with Jesus. If anyone in this manner has seen the glory of Moses by beholding the spiritual Law as a word that refers altogether to Jesus, and if he likewise has seen the wisdom which is mysteriously concealed in the prophets, then he has seen Moses and Elijah in glory, then he has seen them with Jesus.

And a little later:

After the Word has touched them, the disciples open their eyes and see Jesus only, and no one else. Moses or the Law, and Elijah or prophecy, they have become one, one with Jesus, who is the Gospel. Thus it is no longer as it was before; no longer do they remain as three, but the three have become one single entity.[41]

In another discussion Origen adds something further. The gospel story says that Peter wanted to build three tabernacles there, but he did not then know what he was saying. Indeed, Origen writes, 'the Law, the Prophets and the Gospel do not inhabit three tents, but only one, the only tent; that is, the Church of God.'

One figure not mentioned in these profound comments, which I wish I could discuss in much more detail, is an Old Testament character who for Origen and his church points to Jesus in a very special way. He is Joshua, Jesus' namesake, since in Greek both names are spelt in the same way: *Iesous*. In Origen's sermons on the book of Exodus, in chapter 17 he reaches the story of Israel's fight against the Amalekites: 'Then Moses spoke to Joshua and said, "Choose men to fight tomorrow against Amalek." ' When Origen comes to this sentence, he remarks:

Up to this point the Scripture has never anywhere mentioned the blessed name of Jesus. Here for the first time the brightness of the name shines forth. For the first time Moses makes an appeal to Jesus and says to him, "Choose men." Moses calls on Jesus, the Law asks Christ to choose strong men from among the people. Moses cannot choose; it is Jesus alone who can choose strong men; he who has said, "You did not choose me, but I chose you." Indeed, he is the head of those who are chosen, the prince of the strong men; it is he who fought against Amalek. He is the one who enters into the house of the strong man, binds him, and makes himself master of the household.[42]

Origen begins his collection of sermons on Joshua, probably the last book published before his martyrdom, with an introduction about the significance of this book of the Bible.

This significance is not so much to tell us the deeds of Jesus (Joshua) the son of Nun as rather to tell us the mysteries of Jesus my Lord. For it is he who after the death of Moses took over the leadership, he who commanded the camp and who fought against Amalek; and what was indicated there on the mountain, with those outstretched hands, he actualized on the cross, on which in his own person he triumphed over the powers and dominions.

The second sermon deals with a short sentence in the opening part of the Book of Joshua: 'Moses my servant is dead.' The believers must understand what this means in order to see more clearly how Jesus is ruling now.

When you see that the Temple of Jerusalem lies in ruins, that all this liturgy of the Old Testament has ceased, with all these priestly ranks, these festivals and these sacrifices, then you can see what it means that Moses is dead. A new worship has come in place of the old, which in all its details pointed towards the new.

When you see that Christ, our paschal lamb, is slain and that we eat the unleavened bread of purity and truth; when you see that the seed in the good earth of the church brings forth fruit thirty, sixty, and an hundredfold – I mean the widows, the virgins and the martyrs – when you see how the people of Israel are increased in number, the people of those who are born not of blood, nor of the will of man, nor of the will of the flesh, but of God; and when you see the scattered children of God brought together; when you see the people of God celebrate the sabbath, not by refraining from ordinary activities but from words which are sinful; when you see all this, then say, 'God's servant Moses is dead, and Jesus has taken over the leadership.'

The book of Joshua described how Israel conquered the promised land. For Origen, Jesus is the commander of what would later be called 'the church militant'. As a young man, Origen was a witness when the police arrested his father and took him away for a 'trial' in which he was tortured to death. Only by hiding all his clothes was his mother able to prevent Origen from running after his father and sharing his fate. At the time when Origen was delivering this sermon on Joshua, the emperor Decius was engaged in a carefully planned attack on the Christians: his idea was systematically to hamper the leaders of the movement. They would have to fight, not against the power of Rome, but against cowardice and fear and the instinct for self-preservation. This was in fact an extension of the battle which had to be fought by everyone who wanted to follow Joshua and gain a firm footing in the promised land. What does God mean, in this book of the Bible, when he commands, 'Do not leave alive anyone who breathes'? Here is Origen's answer:

Suppose that a feeling of anger arises in my heart. Then it can be that I do not go on to commit the deeds themselves, whether because I do not dare, or because I am fearful of the coming judgment. But that is not enough, the scripture says. You must strive to reach the point that there is no longer any place for even the slightest wave of anger. When the feelings become heated and the mind becomes confused, such agitation is not befitting to a soldier of Jesus, even though it does not result in deeds. This holds true likewise of greed, rancour or any other vice. As for all these passions, the disciple of Jesus must not let them draw one more breath in his heart. If there remains one bad habit or thought, however small, it will gradually grow and will secretly become strong, and then finally (as the Scripture says) make us return to our vomit; for one whom these things overtake, the last state is worse than the first. The prophetic word in the Psalms is directed to this point: blessed is he who takes your little children and dashes them against the rock. The little children of Babylon are nothing but the wicked thoughts which bring disturbances and confusion to the heart. For this is the significance of the word Babel. One must seize these thoughts while they are still small and in their beginning stages, and then dash them to pieces against the rock which is Christ. At his command one must slay them, in order not to leave anything that breathes within us.[43]

A modern reader might find this very moralistic. In fact a great many more, and longer, quotations from Origen would be required to avoid giving a completely false picture of the way in which he interpreted the Bible. Unfortunately, I only have room to add two more comments in conclusion.

First, Origen the preacher was also a biblical scholar, involved in work which we shall find less strange. He devoted an enormous amount of time and energy to the comparative study of the texts of the Bible which were known in his time. The fragments which have come down to us of his Hexaplar, the 'sixfold' Bible, are of incomparable value. In the Hexaplar, in six parallel columns, he wrote down the original text, first in Hebrew letters, then in Greek letters, and then in the four Greek translations current in his time. There were even more versions of the psalms, so his work there spread over into eight columns. When after many years this giant work was eventually finished, it took up approximately six thousand pages and ran to fifty volumes. In addition, Origen continued to search carefully for anything that might shed more light on the original meaning of the biblical texts. He questioned Jewish rabbis about the real meaning of biblical names and from his base in Caesarea explored the geography of the biblical hinterland.

This brings us to a second point. However 'spiritual' his exposition may have been, Origen kept as close as possible to what we would call the 'historicity' of the biblical narratives. For him, everything had happened as it had been recorded. However, what happened then was a pointer to what was taking place now, just as truly, through Jesus and in the church. In this way he defended the reality of revelation and salvation against the 'gnostics' who tended to dissolve it all away into nothingness. At the same time, by means of his 'spiritual' interpretation he was able to defend the Old Testament against the attacks of Marcion and his followers; these read the old book 'according to the letter', and therefore found it to be a document that was valueless once the fullness of revelation had appeared in Christ.

In this connection it should be noted, finally, that for all his scholarship and originality, Origen's sole purpose had been to understand and pass on the ancient traditions of the apostolic church. Most of the prefigurements to which he points in the Old Testament can already be found at an earlier stage, in the New Testament and in writers who preceded him. This is true of Adam and Paradise, Noah and the flood, Abraham and the sacrifice of Isaac, Moses, the exodus through the Red Sea and many other events and personalities. The instruction in the faith which Origen had already received from his father as a boy was full of them. But he will also have added to this stock by means of his studies and his incessant reflection on the biblical texts, all of which seem to have stayed in his memory.

One point is worth noting in connection with this last remark. Joshua 2 tells of the men who were sent to spy out the city of Jericho. They found lodging with a harlot, Rahab, who believed that God would deliver up her country and her city to Israel. She got the two spies to promise that in the destruction of Jerusalem and its inhabitants she and her family would be spared. A red cord hung from the window of her house on the city wall was to be the sign to the Israelite soldiers that her 'house' had to be spared.

Let me now quote a brief passage from Origen. It is evident from it that he knows what Rahab means in Hebrew. Anyone who is familiar with the Bible will recognize texts from Isaiah 49 and 54 in which Jerusalem, personified as a woman, is addressed and is the speaker. Origen says:

Now let us see who this harlot is. She is called Rahab. This name means 'space'. Now what can this space be other than this church of Christ, brought together from sinners who as it were had been practising prostitution? She says, 'The place is too narrow for me; make room for me to dwell in. Who has reared these children for me?' And she receives the answer, 'Set your stakes out farther and enlarge your tent.'[44]

67

Rahab was seen as a 'figure' of the church. Origen develops this further and interprets all the details of the story in a Christian sense. Of course he does this in his own way, but he does not introduce any new element into the content. What he does is to present a part of the church's tradition, which itself in turn has Jewish roots. For Rahab was a Gentile woman who came to recognize Israel's privileges and was able to join the chosen people, indeed was allowed to become the mother of prophets and kings; at the same time she can be seen as an example of the way in which good works are rewarded. Thus Rahab lived on in the estimation of pious Jewish readers of the Bible.

In the New Testament[45] we see that the first Christians took over her person, along with the esteem in which she was held. Matthew gives her a place in the genealogy of Jesus, perhaps in order to demonstrate through her, as through Ruth the Moabitess, that Jesus is the Messiah for all peoples. And Rahab also appears on the scene in the review of the great Old Testament figures of faith in the epistle to the Hebrews: 'By faith Rahab the harlot did not perish with those who were disobedient, because she had given a friendly welcome to the spies.' James also mentions her in connection with faith and works: 'Rahab the harlot was justified by works when she received the messengers and sent them out another way.'

Writing before the end of the first century, Bishop Clement of Rome addressed a kind of pastoral letter to the community in Corinth.[46] Having cited the examples of Noah, Abraham and Lot, he writes: 'The harlot Rahab was saved for her faith and hospitality.' He then tells the broad outlines of the story down to the point when the spies ask Rahab to collect her family together in her house when the Israelites capture the city: 'For everyone found outside this house will perish.' Then they told her, Clement continues,

to prepare a sign: she should hang a red cord from her house. By this they made it manifest that redemption for all who believe and hope in God will come through the blood of the Lord. You see, beloved, how there was not only faith but prophecy in this woman.

The red cord hanging from the window points to the blood of Christ. Others before Clement had probably noted this symbolism

68

already. The much travelled Justin, who became a Christian around the year 130, after trying all the philosophies of his time, also makes the same point in his famous *Dialogue with Trypho the Jew*. He does so in connection with the story of the exodus in which the Israelites were spared from death and destruction by virtue of the blood of the passover lamb which they had smeared on their doorposts. In the same way, says Justin, the blood of Christ will save those who believe in him. This is what was signified by the red cord through which Rahab and her family were saved from destruction. She is the symbol of sinful humanity, who will find deliverance only through faith in the blood of Christ.

Bishop Irenaeus of Lyons, martyred in 202, works out this point in his own way. According to him, Jesus was also thinking of Rahab when he said to the Pharisees, 'Tax-collectors and harlots will enter into the kingdom of God before you.'

Thus much of what Origen presents to the believers in his sermons reflects a pattern of biblical interpretation with which the church had already been familiar for two centuries. Of course he elaborates this tradition with his own emphases, which are then developed further by later generations. For example, he says emphatically that no one should have any illusions about that house of Rahab. Anyone who lived outside it died in the destruction of Jericho, a figure of the world which is perishing. The house of Rahab is the church of Christ: 'If anyone abandons that house, then he becomes responsible for his own ruin.'

As a figure of the saving church, the house of Rahab comes to be set alongside other symbols, like Noah's ark, which is also referred to in the New Testament. And the red cord hanging from the window is set alongside the many other symbols of the passover lamb, and those of other sacrificial rites in the Old Testament. Pieces of wood appearing there can also be seen as pointers to the wood of the cross. A number of sermons by church fathers allude to the wood of Marah. That was the name of the first well which the Israelites reached after their exodus, when they were very thirsty. But the water was so bitter (*marah*) that they could not drink it. In response to Moses' prayer, God showed him a piece of wood. He threw it into the well and the water became sweet. This wood is one of the symbols of the cross. It is what makes the water life-giving.

The water of the Old Law, which is undrinkable when it is read according to the letter, becomes sweet and refreshing when it is touched by the mystery of the cross.

All this makes the Old Testament a contemporary book: read spiritually, it speaks of the great realities in which the Christian lives and of the fulfilment for which he looks. The biblical scholars of these first centuries were always pastors: they preached and gave guidance to believers. They really were 'church fathers'. They helped believers to become familiar with all the ancient figures. So it was only necessary to mention the name of Rahab and any Christian would think of the red cord and the blood of Christ and of the house in which one had to remain in order to escape eternal destruction. The name Jericho reminded them of a place in Palestine and at the same time of the perishable world which is doomed to destruction because of its unbelief. The children of Babylon signified the evil in their own hearts that had to be nipped in the bud.

In this way the Old Testament was just as contemporary as the New. In the quotations from Origen we came across all sorts of allusions to texts from the letters of Paul and the others which speak of the mystery of Christ and of the new dimensions of existence which open up when people believe. The four gospels are not treated in quite the same way. They are narrative in character, like so many books of the Jewish Bible. They too were read spiritually by the church fathers. The facts all occured just as they were described in the gospels; no one doubted that. But at the same time the stories also referred to present experience and future expectation. For the main figure of the gospels was still alive among Christians. 'He not only healed sicknesses and sufferings when these things happened in the flesh (i.e. in historical reality),' wrote Origen, 'but he is still healing them today; he not only came down to men then, but he is still doing this today, and he is present among us.' These words could also have been written by any of the four evangelists, or by a church father from the centuries after Origen. People lived in the belief that

Jesus not only spoke in the synagogue of the Jews in Galilee, but he is still speaking today, in this meeting among us. We are the Jerusalem over which Jesus is still weeping. We are the dead whom he awakens to life. It is his entire church which is a sinner from the beginning of the world and which now throws herself down before him to anoint his feet and then, purified, to stand up. To the believers of all time, and not to Peter alone, he says, 'If I do not wash you, you will have no part in me.' So is it also with his sufferings. Just as in the days of Caiaphas, he is persecuted by false witnesses. From his side there is always the same silence; he does not lift up his voice, but the life of his true disciples speaks for him . . .[47]

In the light of all this, even the texts of the gospels begin to signify much more than is to be read in them at first sight. Here are just two examples from the parables. In these apparently simple stories, the incarnate Wisdom has described the mystery of redemption. In Luke 15, Jesus tells of a woman who has lost one of her ten coins; she lights her lamp and sweeps her house in her search for it, and then invites her neighbours to celebrate when she finds it.

Pope Gregory the Great (590–604) keeps in line with the Christian centuries before him, and also with a saying of Jesus himself, in associating the word 'coin' with an image. According to him, the woman has lost an image, a likeness. Here Jesus is reminding us of man, who was created in God's likeness but has lost this likeness through his own sin.[48]

The lamp which the woman lights points to the mystery of the incarnation. It is clear that in Gregory's time, as in the Palestine of Jesus' day, these lamps were containers for oil which were made from baked clay; a wick protruded from the spout which continued to burn as long as there was oil in the container. 'A lamp is a light in a little earthenware pot; now light in earthenware is the Deity in the flesh.' In Psalm 22 the speaker is the suffering Christ, as he says, 'my strength is dried up like a piece of earthenware'. In the fire that was his suffering, this clay had indeed become hard, and his body acquired new strength in order to rise up again in glory.

Once the woman had lit her lamp, she turned her house inside out. For as soon as the Deity appeared in the flesh, men's consciences fell into confusion. So the lost coin could be found. For the likeness to the creator can only be restored when the conscience is touched.

In this vein, Gregory goes on to explain who are meant by the friends and neighbours of the woman, and what it means that she should have lost just one of her ten coins. To follow this through, though, would require much more space than I have here; for example, I would have to explain about the nine 'choirs' of angels, very familiar to the Christians of Gregory's time, who in their own way were also created in God's image. I would prefer to move on to another example which will mean more to you.

Jesus' parable of the Good Samaritan soon began to be interpreted by Christians in a special way. The interpretation, which I shall go on to describe, was already well-known before the time of Origen and continued to be accepted down the centuries. I first came across this interpretation of the Good Samaritan, like Gregory's interpretation of the lost coin, from readings from the fathers in monastic services.[49] The following description is a kind of standard interpretation which I met during my training, in the preface to a theological manual on the sacraments which was published in Rome in 1920.

In the story of the Good Samaritan, Jesus is supposed to have given an account of his all-embracing work of redemption. *A certain man went down from Jerusalem to Jericho.* This man signifies Adam, father and head of all humanity. In him all have sinned. Jerusalem is the paradisal state of innocence from which this man went down into the changeable condition which is under the dominion of sin, indicated here by Jericho. For the name of this city means 'moon', and the moon with its changeable and sometimes disappearing form is a symbol of the wretched and mortal life here on earth and of all the perishable world.

He fell into the hands of robbers, who not only took away all that he had, but beat him and then went away, leaving him half dead. The robbers represent the devil and his henchmen. Man fell into his hands when he left behind the state of innocence of his own accord. At that time he was robbed of that place near God which had been assigned to him. His reason was no longer capable of ruling over his baser instincts. So there he lay beside the road, half dead, robbed of what God had given him and wounded in the depths of his nature.

A priest happened to come down along this way; he saw him but passed by on the other side. Similarly, a Levite came along past this place, and he saw him and passed by on the other side. These two men signify the priesthood and the sacrificial ministry of the Old Testament. They could not help the robbed and wounded man. After all, it is impossible for sins to be taken away by means of the blood of bulls and goats.

But a Samaritan who was on a journey came in the vicinity, and when he saw him he was moved with compassion. 'Samaritan' comes from a Hebrew word meaning 'someone who watches over, looks after'. This man is a foreigner. He comes from another world. He is the one who existed in the form of God and did not need to regard his equality with God as a thing to be grasped, but for the sake of us men and our salvation came down from heaven, moved by compassion.

He went to him, bound up his wounds, pouring in oil and wine, and he set him on his own donkey, brought him to an inn, and cared for him. The donkey signifies the body in which he came to us, and on it he placed the wounded man; did he not bear our sins in his body on the cross? The bandages with which he bound up the wounds after he had poured oil and wine in them signify the medicines of the sacraments. And the inn is the church which he himself founded on earth in which to provide refreshment for travellers on the way to eternity.

The next day he gave the innkeeper two pieces of money and said, 'Take care of him, and if you have more expenses, I will repay you when I come again.' The next day is the time after his resurrection and before his ascension to the Father. The innkeeper represents the leaders of the church. The two coins which are given to the innkeeper are the gospel and the sacraments of the new Law. Jesus pointed to these when at his departure he charged his disciples to teach and to baptize all nations. They were to do this 'until I return', for this Jesus will return from heaven just as he was taken up there.

8. The Bible in the hands of monastic communities, states and churches

We might call the biblical interpretation of the church fathers 'symbolic'. In that case we could describe it in the terms that Huizinga,

73

the famous Dutch historian, used of the symbolic thinking of the Middle Ages. In the following quotation, when he talks about 'things', including a walnut, one might substitute the biblical words and the realities which they signify.

> Symbolist thought permits of an infinity of relations between things. Each thing may denote a number of distinct ideas by its different special qualities, and a quality may also have several symbolic meanings. The highest conceptions have symbols by the thousand. Nothing is too humble to represent and to glorify the sublime. The walnut signifies Christ; the sweet kernel is His divine nature, the green and pulpy outer peel is His humanity, the wooden shell between is the cross. Thus all things raise the thoughts to the eternal; being thought of as symbols of the highest, in a constant gradation, they are all transfused by the glory of divine majesty.[50]

In biblical interpretation as practised by the church fathers, there resonates in every text what Huizinga calls 'a harmonic accord of symbols'. Through this every biblical term acquires an 'additional value', and along with all the others points to the central mystery of Christ and his church.

Perhaps this is more true of the book of Psalms than of most other parts of the Bible. Bishop Augustine, who died in 430, regularly preached expository sermons on the Psalms. A number of these were published round about the year 417. This book, *Enarrationes in psalmos*, is one of the longest of his works, twice as long as his famous book *The City of God*. Careful investigation has shown that 119 of these sermons were given extemporaneously and taken down by secretaries; in addition, he dictated 86 expositions at home to make the volume more complete. In the expositions taken down by secretaries, Augustine sometimes confesses that he has prepared to speak on a psalm other than the one which has just been read by the lector. Then he improvises. Anyone who is at all familiar with his style and is not frightened off by certain expressions which are characteristic of the time can only marvel at the certainty with which Augustine sees a reference to Christ in every verse. When Augustine uses this name he thinks at one and the same time of both a person and a world-wide fellowship. For example, the title of Psalm 61 says that it is a prayer of David. For Augustine, Christ, the Son of David, is praying here; the head and members, all believers throughout the whole earth.[51]

In the speaker in this psalm we must recognize ourselves and no one else. By ourselves I do not mean only those who are present here, but all of us over the whole world from east to west. And to show that it really is the voice of all of us, he speaks as though it were one single man. But it is not one single man, but in this one man our unity is speaking. For through Christ we are all one man. The head of this one man is in heaven, but the members toil here on earth. Note what he says in reference to this existence of toil.

This is already evident where the psalmist (in the Latin translation which Augustine uses) says that he cries to God 'from the ends of the earth'. This cannot be an individual. It can only be the whole church, which is addressing God here from the depth of her afflictions. All members of Christ must follow the course of his life, including his sufferings. As he overcame them, so too will the Christians who follow in his footsteps. A little later, the Latin text of this psalm goes on: 'You set me high upon the rock.'

Therefore it is no wonder that in the midst of the afflictions he cries from the ends of the earth. And why is he not overcome? High on the rock you set me. Indeed, now we understand who it is that is crying from the ends of the earth. Think of the gospel: On this rock I will build my church. Thus it is she whom he willed to build upon the rock, she who is crying over all the earth. But in that case, who has become this rock on which the church can be built? Listen to Paul: Now the rock was Christ. Thus it is on him that we are built. Therefore this rock on which we are built was earlier buffeted by wind, flood and rain, when Christ was tested by the devil. This is the foundation on which he willed to establish you. Our cry therefore is not a fruitless outcry, but it is heeded. Great is the confidence in which we rest. High on the rock you set me.

I shall resist the temptation to go on quoting from this 'exposition' in which Augustine time and again gives sublime expression to what constitutes the heart of Christian experience. The same character can be found in innumerable passages in this priceless book of *Enarrationes*. What I am concerned with is the role of the psalms in the prayers of the church, and above all of those called to prayer, including the monastic orders. The solemn singing of the psalms at all hours of the day and night determined the atmosphere in which innumerable of them became the highest vehicles for contemplation.

So it went on down the centuries. When the Spaniard Dominic, at the beginning of the thirteenth century, broke through the old monastic forms and founded religious communities to serve as bases for preaching to the people, he maintained the meditative recitation of the psalms. He asked his colleagues to learn Paul's letters off by heart, as good representatives of 'the apostle' in a modern age, which had seen profound alterations to the structures of society. He said nothing about the book of Psalms. He took it for granted that they would already know the psalms by heart. On their month-long journeys, crossing the Europe of those days again and again on foot, he and his companions would recite the psalms, the prayers of the Christ in whose continuing activity they knew that their own life-work was incorporated.

In the preface to his 'exposition of the Psalms of David', written about 1253, Thomas Aquinas, a disciple of Dominic, shows in his own way why the book of Psalms plays such an important role in the life of the church. Thomas' method is systematic. According to him, the 'matter' contained in the psalms coincides with the whole of theology. All the four great themes of theology are treated in it: creation, salvation, restoration through the incarnation and the final consummation. On the third point he remarks: 'All that concerns that restoration through the incarnation is treated so clearly in this book of the Bible that it almost resembles a gospel rather than a prophecy.' This treatment of all the themes of theology is also the reason why 'the psalter is the most extensively used book in the church; it in fact contains the whole of scripture'. And a little later, 'The subject-matter of this book is Christ and his people.'[52]

As for literary forms in the Bible, one finds narrative form in the historical books; hortatory, admonitory and mandatory form in the laws, the prophetic books and the didactic books; and discussion, above all in Job and in Paul. But there is also the form of prayer and praise. This is used in the Psalter: 'All that is expressed in the other biblical books in the above-mentioned forms is found here in the style of praise and prayer.'

Despite the nature of its conceptuality, the theology of Thomas was deeply rooted in biblical soil. With his successors, we see the tree increasingly cut off from these roots. All that is left is a fruitless game of playing with ideas; to put it in the style of the church fathers, there are branches without leaves and blooms in which birds can no longer build a nest. Only in a few monastic communities is Bible reading in the style of Origen and Augustine still a well from which people draw living water.

In 1501, Erasmus attempted once again to make this well accessible to the ordinary believer. At that time he wrote his *Handbook for the Christian Soldier*, which was printed in 1503 and particularly after 1510 was widely distributed and much read, before long in several translations into the vernacular. According to Erasmus, Christians ought to learn to read the scriptures in the same way as Augustine, Ambrose, Jerome and especially Origen, who for him held pride of place among the interpreters of the Bible. The believing reader was to search for the deeper significance behind the literal meaning of the biblical texts. 'The Spirit' sought to reach him through 'the flesh' of the letter and to affect him in the only thing that mattered, the mystery of Christ. Of course that held true for the Old Testament. What was the point of reading about the formation of Adam from clay and of Eve from Adam's rib, and all the rest, if not to seek something more behind them? What was the difference between reading Old Testament books like Kings and Judges and the historical works of Livy if one paid no attention to allegorical meaning? Everywhere, and especially in the Old Testament, it was necessary to minimize the flesh of the scriptures and to work out the spiritual, mystical sense.

That was also true of the gospels. There, too, we have flesh and spirit. It is Christ himself who says that the flesh profits nothing and that only the spirit gives life. 'I surely would not have dared to say this in such strong terms. It would have been sufficient to say that the flesh indeed does have some value, but the spirit has much more. Now the Truth himself says it so strongly: "The flesh profits nothing."' At one point Erasmus cites a whole series of biblical

77

texts which speak of springs that bring refreshment and healing for men. In these we may see a pointer to the mysteries of the scriptures: 'What does the water that is hidden deep in the earth signify, other than the mystery that is enclosed within the letter?'[53]

Historians differ over the influence of Erasmus on the Reformation. It seems to me that the method of reading the Bible that he advocates will still be practised for some time to come in pietist circles. But it presupposes a developed capacity for symbolic thinking, and the intellectual atmosphere of the centuries after Erasmus was not conducive to this. However, in our time it is not just anybody or everybody who will declare without further ado that 'symbolic' reading of the Bible is no longer possible for modern man.

So much for the first of the three methods of interpretation that I wanted to outline in this chapter. In the fourth century, yet another way of interpreting the Bible came into vogue alongside this one. This was the more or less literal use of the Old Testament. With the emperor Constantine, who died in 336, Christianity became the state religion. After the fall of the Roman Empire we see the beginning of what was soon to become 'Christendom'. This term carries with it the idea that the whole life of society is based on Christian principles. The population of the new Europe is the 'people of God'. Here on a large scale was what the Old Testament said of the people of Israel. Israel, as a nation, was destined to embody in its national structures the demands of the covenant, and in particular the exclusive worship of the true God. These structures were to protect it against the influence of the heathen nations round about.

At an early period, shortly after the time of Constantine, Christian fanatics appealed to Deuteronomy 13, with its harsh rules against anyone who worships another deity, or attempts to lead members of the nation into such idolatry. These rules were now taken to be binding upon Christian emperors.

One of the great modern champions of the ecumenical movement, the Dominican Yves Congar, has produced a large number of examples of the influence which the literal application of the Old Testament had on the life of society in various areas of early Christendom.[54] He cites the development of a hierarchy of clergy of differing rank, whose primary function is to conduct liturgical services, and for whom rites of consecration were worked out in line with the prescriptions of Moses. Another instance is the assessment of tithes for the support of these clergy. In the eighth century, kings were anointed according to the example of Saul and David. At that time people also began to consecrate churches with a ceremonial following the laws of Exodus and Leviticus, with sprinkling, anointing and incense. In Christian Ireland in the seventh century the observance of Sunday was modelled on that of the sabbath.

One of the court theologians of Charlemagne (768–814) was called Alcuin. Those who have done research into his writings on politics and society have demonstrated that four-fifths of the terms which he used come from the Old Testament. For him, Charlemagne is the new Josiah, called to restore the worship of the true God in all its purity. Most of all, however, Alcuin calls Charlemagne the chosen David. The conclusion of Deuteronomy 17 was held up as a mirror before Charlemagne and many Christian rulers after him. Because of that, however, the wars which they fought were called holy wars. Whenever people with pacifist views appealed to the new spirit which Christ had brought, the theologians would refer them to Jesus, who had spoken so approvingly of the officer in Capernaum, and to Cornelius in Acts 10, who was also a soldier, or to the fact that while John the Baptist gave all kinds of admonitions to the soldiers who came to him, he did not denounce their profession.

Congar has also made a study of the different applications of a saying addressed by God to Jeremiah when he called him to act as a prophet: 'Behold, I have set you over nations and kingdoms, to pluck up and to break down, and to plant.'[55] He shows that in the early centuries bishops and priests saw their own pastoral task expressed in this text, often in combination with words of Jesus to Peter. According to a biographer in the eighth century, a man like Pope Gregory the Great had put them into practice because he had indeed 'pulled up the roots of evil and destroyed them everywhere, and planted and built up virtues'. Later the saying began to function to the advantage of the popes, to whom God was supposed to have given the fullness of spiritual and temporal power.

A similar use of the Bible is to be seen in the famous text about the two swords. A study of this subject begins with a problem which Charlemagne posed in a letter to his theologian Alcuin. According to the evangelist Luke, just before his arrest Jesus commanded his disciples to sell their cloaks and to buy a sword. When they answered that they had two swords, he said, 'That is enough'. Peter must have used one of these two swords to cut off Malchus' ear. But then Jesus says, 'Put your sword into its sheath, for those who use the sword shall die by the sword.' 'How can this be?' asks Charlemagne. 'If the sword is the word of God, and if the Lord, in his command to buy a sword, meant that word of God, how then can one say that all who receive the word of God shall perish through that word of God?' Charlemagne had stumbled on a contradiction in the gospels and he did not find a solution to it with the help of a symbolic meaning. He did not know that the question had already been discussed by many interpreters of the scriptures in the centuries before him, any more than he could suspect that in the centuries after him the text about the two swords would come to serve as a weapon in passionate disputes between popes and emperors about the supreme power.

Biblical texts also played a major role in mobilizing Christendom for the crusades, and in the moral justification of them.[56] Christians countered the *jihad*, the 'holy war' of Islam, which at that time posed a fatal threat to them, with their own holy war against the heretics and unbelievers. One of the aims of the crusades was the conquest of the Holy Land. The book of Joshua provides specific guidelines for the campaign, even to details like the presence of priests in the armies of the crusaders. The stories of the Maccabees' fight against the armies of the heathen also served as models. The Jerusalem of the prophets and the psalms, from the time of Paul's letter to the Galatians located in the world 'above', now once again became the earthly city, to which the crusaders would bring deliverance and glory. They were the ones who would fulfil Isaiah 60, and texts like Zechariah 12. Jesus had said that Jerusalem would be oppressed by the Gentiles 'until the times of the Gentiles should be fulfilled'. The crusaders were now bringing about this fulfilment: in accordance with Jesus' words, they had denied themselves and taken up the cross.

Nowadays people like to connect the history of the crusades with the invasion from the west to which Palestine has been subjected in our time. There is, however a subsequent Christian enterprise which offers a better parallel in both the method of colonization and the biblical justification for it: the Spanish conquest of America.

In 1513 the Spanish king Ferdinand appointed a commission of theologians. Some Dominicans had championed the rights of the natives in the new world. At that time an expensive fleet lay at anchor ready to depart on a new expedition. King Ferdinand, however, would not let it set sail until the theologians had found a moral basis for their war against the Indians. The commission allowed itself to be convinced by the biblical arguments put forward by Enciso.[57]

He defended the thesis that God had entrusted the Indies to Spain, just as he had given the promised land to the Jews:

Moses sent Joshua to the inhabitants of Jericho, the first city in the promised land of Canaan, to demand that they abandon their city because it belonged to the people of Israel, in view of the fact that God had given it to them. And when the people of Jericho did not give up their city, Joshua besieged them and killed them all, except for a woman who had protected his spies. And after this Joshua conquered the entire land of Canaan by armed force; many were killed, and the prisoners of war were made slaves and served the people of Israel. And all this was done by the will of God, because they were idolators.

This last point was a very clever move on the part of Enciso. He knew the aversion of the Spaniards to any form of idolatry. Evidently no one doubted his interpretation of Israel's ancient history. He completed his plea by explaining that the Pope, who was God's representative, had given the Indies to Spain and along with them the idolatrous inhabitants of these lands, with the intention that the Catholic king should introduce Christianity there. Therefore, he said,

it is perfectly justifiable that the king should send men to demand of these idolatrous Indians that they yield their land to him; for it is given to him by the Pope. If the Indians are not willing to do this, he may justly wage war on them, kill them, and make slaves of the prisoners of war, just as Joshua treated the inhabitants of the land of Canaan.

81

Bartolomeo de las Casas, who was drawn to the New World as a colonist in 1502, began from 1514 onwards to devote himself entirely to the battle for the human rights of the Indians. Contrary to public opinion in the Spanish empire, he continued to maintain that the Indians were men in the full sense of the word; he even defended what must have seemed a monstrous point of view, holding that in certain respects the Indians were more civilized than the Spaniards who had invaded their land with violence. He wrote important books on the culture and the history of the people of central America. In them he described the ancient temples in Mexico, which according to him equalled the pyramids of Egypt, a fact rediscovered in our century by archaeologists and now confirmed by rich tourists. A high point in the life of this great defender of the defenceless was a public dispute with Sepulveda which took place in Valladolid in 1551.

Sepulveda found a biblical argument in Jesus' parable of the wedding feast. In it the Lord says, 'Compel them to come in.' Therefore the Spaniards might use force against the natives. Las Casas had to be very careful in answering this argument. For emperors and popes had also used it, and the Inquisition was lying in wait. He explained that this text did not refer to external compulsion, but to 'an internal compulsion by the inspiration of God and by the ministry of his angels'. For this interpretation he could appeal to one of the great church fathers.

Alongside 'figurative' interpretation and the literal and practical application of the Bible, a third usage may be mentioned: people use texts to prove that their doctrinal views are correct. This usage came strongly to the fore after the disintegration of Christendom. During the Counter-Reformation, the church of Rome firmly shut itself in behind its own fortifications. Protestant churches grew up around Luther, Calvin, Zwingli and others. Very soon the new movements solidified into more or less formally structured church communities, and their doctrine solidified in confessional writings. As a result of this, one and the same biblical text could provoke directly opposite reactions. When a Catholic hears Jesus' words to Peter, 'Upon this rock I will build my church,' he thinks of the Pope and of St Peter in Rome. A Protestant realizes that whatever else the saying may mean, it cannot refer to the papacy.

82

When the 'age of reason' dawned in the eighteenth century, the churches began to have difficulties with their old doctrinal positions about holy scripture and faith. A friend recently showed me a book written by a Professor P. van Limburg Brouwer of Groningen, published in 1847. This man had taught classics, but felt himself deeply affected by developments in the Dutch Protestant churches of the time. There was a struggle between a group which wanted to bring the Christian faith into harmony with reason and feeling, and in this connection wanted to set the inspiring figure of Christ at the centre of the life of faith, and other groups who wanted to hold more or less strictly to the old formulations. In his book, *Het leesgezelschap van Diepenbeek*, van Limburg Brouwer describes the effects of these ecclesiastical controversies on a small village community. It is a kind of satire, obviously written with pleasure and with a touch of malicious satisfaction. I much enjoyed reading it.[58] But in a reader who has the temperament of the author of Ecclesiastes, or in one who is somewhat pessimistic by nature, it can raise the question: were not the conflicts then exactly as they are now? Is there really anything new under the sun? It seems to me that since 1840 developments have taken place which put the focal point of conflict elsewhere.

II · The Historical Approach

Round about the year 1800, many European historians began to feel that they had been utterly mistaken in their understanding of certain periods of the past. They felt the urge to use every means possible to search out 'the facts as they really were'. One of their most typical representatives is Berthold Niebuhr, the German statesman who started his *History of Rome* in 1912.[59] Until that time, the earliest history of Rome had been passed down from generation to generation as it had originally been written by Titus Livy, whose extensive history first appeared round about the beginning of the Christian era. He told of the founding of Rome in 753 BC by Romulus and Remus, of the first seven kings, and so on. Niebuhr demonstrated that the narrative presented by Livy was to a large extent built on legends, and he even pointed to what he called 'mythical' elements in it.

Niebuhr's book made a critical examination of a piece of ancient history. He posed such questions as, 'Where did the author get his information? What is the historical value of his sources? What was Livy's aim in writing? What were his assumptions and his prejudices?'

This need to trace things as far back as possible had already become the pattern long before in other areas of scholarship, especially in the natural sciences. However, such an approach was virtually new in the sphere of history. Hence the thoroughgoing investigation made by Niebuhr gave a powerful impetus to the development of what is called 'critical history study'.

Should such study call a halt at the boundaries of the sacred territory of the Bible? After all, this book too is a document from

84

antiquity. Like Livy's history, it too contains numerous stories from earlier times. May questions like those of Niebuhr also be asked in connection with the Bible? Is it permissible to investigate the origin of the stories in the Bible and to test the historical reliability of its writers also?

Many Christians declared their conviction that it was not. It was permissible to use the help of scientific scholarship to trace the original wording of the biblical text (textual criticism) and to grasp the meaning of it as fully as possible (Semitic and Greek philology). From the sixteenth century onwards this had been done on an ever-increasing scale. No objection to these studies could be raised from the perspective of faith. But for a believing Christian, at any rate, there could be no thought of the use of 'historical criticism', as Niebuhr had applied it to Livy, in connection with the Bible. This conclusion followed from the conviction that the Bible was God-given, 'inspired' down to the last detail. So the Bible is free from any error. God cannot lie nor deceive. Now what is called 'historical criticism' begins from the assumption that in this connection there is something to investigate. It assumes that the actual course of events could have been other than the biblical narratives give us to understand. So there might be untruths in the Bible. By taking this as a starting point, such an investigation undermines the divine authority of the Bible, and with it the faith that is put in the Bible.

That was the conviction of a great many Christians in the church. So protests increased in number and intensity when biblical scholars began to use the new instrument of 'historical criticism' in their research. Professor J. Lutz, a clergyman who from 1834 until his death in 1844 was Professor of Biblical Studies in Basle, was concerned about 'the steadily widening gulf between the beliefs of people in the church and scholarly interpretation of the Bible'. Forty years later, one of the greatest biblical scholars of his time, Julius Wellhausen, asked to be transferred from the theological faculty to the faculty of philosophy. In a letter dated 5 April 1882, he reminded the Prussian Minister of Culture that his request of two years earlier had still not been approved.[60] In this letter he wrote: 'I became a theologian because I was interested in the scientific investigation of the Bible. It has only gradually become evident to me that a professor of theology also has the practical task of preparing students for service in the

Protestant Church, and that in this practical task I have fallen short. Indeed, in spite of all reserve on my part, I am in fact making my hearers unfit for their ministry.' This last remark is worth noting. We have seen that the 'canonization' of the Torah, and with it the idea of 'divine inspiration', was connected with the organization of the Jews into a clearly segregated community. Could the resistance of the official churches to historical investigation, which seemed to deny the possibility of inspiration, be connected with their own concern to stand apart as a community, as a 'true church'? Perhaps we shall be able to say more about this question when we have looked at a few instances which show how profoundly the new approach affected the pattern of thought with which Christians had been familiar since the beginnings of the church.

1. Moses and the Pentateuch

All down the centuries it had been thought that the first five books of the Bible had been written by Moses, under divine inspiration. They formed one large work, before the time of Christ already divided into five (*pente*) scrolls (*teuchos*), hence 'Pentateuch'. With the exception of solitary critical spirits here and there, no one had doubted this idea prior to the nineteenth century. There was no reason at all to do so. The second of the five books, Exodus, begins with Moses' birth and he remains the chief figure in the story, even in the following books, down to the fifth, in which there is an account of his death. Moses writes that he is a descendant of Levi, one of the twelve sons of the patriarch Jacob, who himself was a grandson of Abraham. The latter's forefathers were known by name back to, and including, the first, Adam. So what Moses wrote in the first book, Genesis, about events which had happened long before his birth, he could have known from oral tradition. Besides, he himself describes how intimately he talked with God, as friend with friend. So he could know as it were at first hand how the creation of the world had taken place.

Moreover, Moses relates more than once that he had set down in writing the facts which he had experienced and witnessed, and furthermore that he recorded the laws which God had dictated to him. Alongside these statements made by Moses himself, in other books of the Old Testament there are references on several occasions to the lawbook that he had produced, 'the Law of Moses'. However, what carried the most weight of all was the declaration of Christ, who said to the Jews, 'If you believed Moses, you would believe me, for he wrote of me. But if you do not believe his writings, how will you believe my words?'[61]

Hence the shock which went through the churches when biblical scholars declared: 'This cannot be true. Moses cannot have written the first five books of the Bible. It is a historical impossibility.'

Those who could take in their arguments calmly were soon convinced, especially if they were familiar with insights which had found acceptance earlier. In 1753, Jean Astruc, the physician of the French royal court, who had enough free time to concern himself with other sciences as well, wrote a book with the provocative title, 'Conjectures about the documents which Moses appears to have used in the writing of the book of Genesis'. He had already seen that various 'hands' could be at work in the book of Genesis. 'Now that is simply a historical impossibility,' said the biblical scholars of a century later. Such an enormous work as the Pentateuch could not have been written in about 1400 BC, certainly not with the aid of already existing 'documents'. For most of the stories and collections of laws which form the Pentateuch can only have arisen in a highly developed society. It is inconceivable that the 'founder' of Israel could have produced such a work on his own, in a social and cultural void, in the wilderness in which he is said to have spent the last forty years of his life, which were also the first years of Israel's existence as a nation. Moreover, the Pentateuch did not yet exist in its present form even during the reigns of David, Solomon and the kings who followed them, during the time of the great prophets or during the Babylonian exile. For not only do reliable biblical accounts of these centuries say nothing about the Pentateuch; beside that, much of the history is utterly incomprehensible if we assume that the Pentateuch did exist. However, if we accept that the 'documents' of which the work is made up came into being during the course of this history, then we can also gain a clear insight into the development of Israel's religion and the emergence of the Pentateuch.

This clear insight was provided primarily by Julius Wellhausen, the brilliant German biblical scholar whom we have already mentioned. From 1870 onwards he wrote books and articles putting forward his theory about the development of the Pentateuch. He argued like this. The foundation for the Pentateuch was laid shortly after the time of Solomon, in about 850 BC, by an author from the kingdom of Judah whose name is unknown to us. He wrote a history which began with the creation of Adam and Eve in Paradise and their fall, Cain's murder of his brother, the flood and the tower of Babel. After that came stories about Abraham, Isaac and Jacob, the stay of Jacob's sons in Egypt, the exodus under the leadership of Moses, the appearance of God on Mount Sinai, some laws, and the journey through the wilderness which ended with Moses' death. About a century later, in 750 BC or thereabouts, an author from the northern kingdom wrote a similar history, which began with the life story of Abraham. After the fall of the northern kingdom, these two books were combined into one; that happened around the years 650 BC. The law book which was discovered in the Temple in Jerusalem during the reign of king Josiah in 621 BC corresponds to the book of Deuteronomy, the last part of Moses' work. In the middle of the next century, around 500 BC, it was combined with the larger historical work mentioned above. During and after the exile the priests worked out a large number of liturgical regulations, and on the basis of liturgical calendars they worked out a chronological system into which they fitted the history of Israel and of mankind since the creation. About the year 400 BC these elements were combined with the larger historical work and Deuteronomy to form the complex whole which we call 'the books of Moses' or the Pentateuch.

The theory seemed utterly shocking. Fancy thinking that the Law of Moses had come into being a thousand years later than people had believed all through the centuries, and had not been written by the greatest inspired figure of the Old Testament, but by unknowns from a much later time! Wellhausen contended that because these unknown writers lived so many centuries after Moses, they could not have had much reliable information about his person and his work. So the clear picture of Moses given in the Pentateuch must be attributed to the imagination of later generations. According to Wellhausen, nothing at all can be said with any certainty about the patriarchs of Israel; the only knowledge we have is what these authors, living in 850 or 750 BC, thought of their distant ancestors of a thousand years earlier. Thus Wellhausen and all these other modernists flatly rejected the church's dogma of inspiration, not only by denying that Moses had anything to do with the writing of the Pentateuch, but also by assuming that the book was full of lies. Furthermore, it followed from their view that Christ had lied when he said that Moses had written about him. That was nothing less than blasphemy.

Indeed, it was held, the whole theory was simply a product of unbelievers. Those who held it were constantly talking about 'historical impossibilities', about 'clarifying the historical course of events', and so on. As though such overwhelming acts of God as the exodus and the revelation on Sinai and the inspiration of Moses could be measured by our sinful standards! As though any attitude were appropriate here other than one of reverence and gratitude, putting all questions of human curiosity to silence!

Believers in the church regarded Wellhausen as antichrist. He suffered severely under attacks from this direction, some of which were more than unchristian. The intense indignation was a mark of the fear that this new approach would undermine the entire system of Christian dogma. So the new theory also set off an avalanche of articles, books and pamphlets, in which all the arguments were supposedly refuted with a greater or lesser degree of skill.

The Church of Rome, with its powerful stress on authoritative teaching, soon reacted with an unequivocal rejection of the theory. A few Roman Catholic biblical scholars had said that they could accept the new view of the Pentateuch. They felt that this view need not conflict with the divine inspiration of the Bible, as long as this doctrine were understood correctly. In Holland, it was defended by a priest from Limburg, Henri Poels, who was both intelligent and energetic. He had become acquainted with the new historical method during his studies at Louvain. He defended it in a long article entitled 'The Origin of the Pentateuch', which was published in a journal called *De Katholiek* in December 1898. It was intended to be the first in a series, but the others never appeared. As early as the beginning of 1899, the bishop of Haarlem presented 'the Poels case' to Rome. As a result, this biblical scholar was debarred from taking up the professorship in the seminary at Roermond for which he had been destined, and was appointed chaplain at Venlo.[62]

The resistance of the Roman Catholic theologians was understandable. They regarded the new view of the Pentateuch as an expression of 'modernism', the name they gave to any current thinking governed by the recognition that everything, including religion, is subject to historical evolution, and hence to change. This insight seemed irreconcilable with the Catholic faith as it had taken shape in the church of Rome. The church regarded itself as the guardian of revealed truth which had been entrusted to it by God and was fixed in dogmas, unchangeable formulations which were valid for all time. Concepts like historical development and change seemed to be as much in conflict with this position as did the introduction of personal experience and feelings into such matters of truth, an approach to which the modernists attached a good deal of importance.

In 1905 the Papal Biblical Commission, established in 1902 to give guidance to biblical study and interpretation in the church, began to issue a series of norms for teaching, in the form of answers to doubts that were presented to them.[63] They formulated these doubts (*dubia*) so carefully that the answer to them was always a simple yes or no, thus leaving nothing to be desired as far as clarity was concerned.

The question of the Pentateuch was taken up as early as June 1906. The meaning of the yes-and-no answers to the four questions amounted to this: 'The arguments of present-day historical criticism are not strong enough to overthrow the centuries-old tradition which regards Moses as the author of the Pentateuch; it is possible that he made use of oral and written sources and that he entrusted to secretaries the actual task of setting it down in writing; slight variations, additions and glosses (though these, of course, will have been inspired) may have found their way into the text during the centuries of their transmission; but the substance of the work goes back to Moses himself.'

Catholic biblical scholars soon made their objections. They could understand that the church authorities wanted to protect the mass of the faithful from any sudden encounter with the new views which might needlessly confuse them. But surely the Pope did not mean to put an end to the open and scientific approach being made by serious investigators?

'I intend precisely that,' replied Pius X in a declaration made on

18 November 1907: in conscience, every Catholic was to submit to all pronouncements of the Biblical Commission, already made or yet to be made; he would be guilty of a grave sin before God if he attacked them in any way, verbally or in writing.

That put an end to all research in Roman Catholic circles. Anyone who wrote anything showing traces of the new theory about the Pentateuch was immediately called to order and sometimes removed from office, with dramatic and often painful consequences.

The effects of all this were felt in the training of priests throughout the world. If students heard anything at all about the Pentateuch, it would be almost exclusively the proofs for Mosaic authorship, and a detailed refutation of the arguments put forward by 'rationalists' or 'unbelieving criticism'. Those Catholics who began their study for the priesthood with some interest in holy scripture soon lost it again as a result of this defensive approach, which was also characteristic of the official treatment of other parts of the Bible.

The embargo on critical views was not lifted until 1943. The upheavals caused by the war did not prevent Roman Catholics from celebrating a jubilee: fifty years earlier in his encyclical *Providentissimus Deus*, Pope Leo XIII had laid down guidelines for a modern interpretation of the Bible. Half a century later, Pius XII was Pope; he had placed his confidence in Father Bea, a Jesuit and a great authority on modern biblical scholarship. Bea made use of his position to get the Pope to write a new encyclical, connected with the jubilee; its opening words were *Divino afflante Spiritu* (Through the divine inspiration of the spirit). This letter contained an urgent recommendation to Catholic biblical scholars to use all the modern critical methods, as well as the increasing amount of information provided by excavations and newly deciphered texts from the ancient Near East, in determining the meaning of the sacred texts. The letter explicitly protected Roman Catholic scholars from attacks made on them by orthodox believers:

All other children of the church must remember that they must judge the efforts of these stalwart labourers in the vineyard of the Lord (the biblical scholars!) not only with justice and fairness, but also with the greatest love. They must avoid the unhealthy tendency to think that everything that is new must for that reason be contested or be regarded with suspicion.

A little later, it spoke of the freedom of Catholic interpreters as

> this true freedom of the children of God which both faithfully adheres to the church's teaching and gratefully accepts and uses, as a gift of God, all that profane sciences have provided.

After the war, the salutary effects of Pius' encyclical of 1943 could be seen in all kinds of books and articles. The Catholic interpreters of the Bible felt that they had been freed from the heavy pressure which had prevented them from passing on their findings to others. Instead of presenting a cramped defence of the Mosaic authorship of the Pentateuch, in which they themselves had long since ceased to believe, seminary professors could now devote their time to the true significance of the Pentateuch. Of course, to begin with, only a few were really up to the task: they had not been trained for this kind of biblical interpretation.

The statement in the encyclical about the freedom of the children of God went on to refer to faithful adherence to the church's tradition. It was now permissible to apply historical criticism to the Bible. Was it not an obvious course to go on to apply it to later, non-biblical formulations of the faith? Had not the dogmas and the developed system of doctrine constructed upon them developed historically, and were they not therefore subject to alteration? In 1951, Pius XII wrote his encyclical *Humani Generis*, which on certain points seemed once again to restrict the freedom of investigation which had been granted in 1943. But *Divino afflante* had done its work, and remained an important factor in the stormy developments which led to the Second Vatican Council.

The Second Vatican Council was called primarily at the instigation of Pope John, who brought to the Vatican a robust common sense as a result of his peasant background, and a marked interest in history which had been prompted by his later career. However, the situation towards which his initiative was directed had been well prepared for in advance. It was certainly no coincidence that Father Bea, the man behind the encyclical of 1943, and now a cardinal, was given the task of drawing together the various ecumenical endeavours.

92

The dispute over Moses and the Pentateuch was no less intense in the world of the Protestant churches. There, however, it was carried on in a number of different settings, and the teaching authority that defended the tradition was not embodied in any one individual, such as the Pope. Those called to give judgment were corporate bodies, like church councils, assemblies, or synods. These also called ministers and theologians to order, and sometimes relieved them of their posts, with all the dramatic consequences which ensue.

The more a Protestant church was oriented on the past in its thinking, the later the change was to come. In 1952, an introduction to the books of the Old Testament by Professor G. Aalders of the Free University of Amsterdam was published under the title *Oud-Testamentische Kanoniek*.[64] In a very elaborate chapter on 'the law', he came to the conclusion that the bulk of the Pentateuch must have been written by Moses himself, or at least under his direction, and that documents from an earlier time must have been used in the process. Only one or two sections of the book were added after the death of Moses. The Pentateuch must have been known to the Israelites 'virtually in its present form' in the time of the judges. The final editing of the work must have taken place in 'the reign of Saul, or at the latest in the years when David was king in Hebron'. This interpretation enables Aalders to retain all the other data of the Bible in the most literal sense, even the solemn declaration by Christ mentioned above. In his view it is better to assign to the word *grammasin* in the Greek text the ordinary meaning of 'letters'; here the Saviour is contrasting his own spoken words with the written words of Moses. 'If you do not believe what he wrote . . .' In that case, Moses need only have written the bulk of the Pentateuch and not the entire work.

It is a testimony to the rapidity of developments that this view is now a thing of the past, even among the theological students of the Dutch Reformed Church. After all, were they to retain such a view, when it came to the study of modern commentaries and handbooks on the Old Testament and works on historical developments in ancient Israel, they would have to note their objections on almost every page.

93

2. Isaiah and his book

The gospels, the book of Acts and the epistles contain almost more references to Isaiah than to any other book in the Old Testament. That is why Isaiah is revered as the greatest of the prophets. God allowed him to catch a clearer glimpse than others of the great divine work that was to be performed at the end of time. Isaiah had a vision of Emmanuel, born of a maiden, the child who at his birth awakened joy because the government of the world was set on his shoulders ... He also had a vision of the man who, endowed with the seven-fold gifts of the spirit, was the servant or slave of the Lord who took upon himself the proclamation of God's will, became a victim of man's sinfulness, and was offered up by God as a sin-offering for the many ... Isaiah also spoke of the glory of the heavenly Jerusalem, the destruction of death at the end of time, and of many other realities with which the Christian was familiar.

That is why the commentary written by the German scholar Bernard Duhm and published in 1893 caused such a great shock. In his view, sayings of the great prophet Isaiah (who lived around 740 BC) were to be found only in the first part of the book. Chapters 40–55 had been composed by an unknown writer who was active about 150 years later, during the Babylonian exile. He also argued that Isaiah 56–66 was the work of a variety of authors, most of whom wrote after the return from exile in 538 BC.

A storm of protest broke loose. First Moses, God's confidant and the inspired lawgiver, had become the target of critics; now it was Isaiah, the greatest of the inspired prophets. Duhm argued in a sober, matter-of-fact way that a prophet was a sane, sensible man who had a message for his contemporaries. What use had they for descriptions of a situation which would not be realized for another 150 years? And what concern did they have for a Messiah to come in a future that was even more remote?

For believers within the church, this common-sense approach was proof enough that the new school to which Duhm belonged had broken completely with the Christian faith. After all, the fulfilment of prophecy was one of the foundations of the faith. The new assessment of the book of Isaiah denied even the possibility of prophecy, understood as God-given knowledge of future events. True, Duhm did not make this point explicitly in his writing, but those believers who picked up his enormous work were aware that the denial of the supernatural could easily be read between its lines.

On 28 June 1908, the Papal Biblical Commission reacted with an answer to some *dubia* which had been presented to it. Because the text is rather shorter than that on the Pentateuch issued two years before, I shall give the translation for the interested reader who is prepared to struggle with long sentences.

Dubium I
Is it permissible to teach that the predictions which appear in the book of Isaiah – and elsewhere in the Scriptures – are not genuine predictions, but that they are stories which were invented after the events, or, if it must be acknowledged that something was announced before it happened, that the prophet did not announce this in advance on the basis of a supernatural revelation from God who knows the future, but on the basis of what he conjectured, thanks to a fortuitous discernment and his own keenness of understanding?
Answer: No.

Dubium II
Can one combine the thesis according to which Isaiah and other prophets spoke only of events of their own time or about things that would happen not long thereafter with the certain fact of the predictions which have to do with the Messiah and the events of the end, which the same prophets wrote far in advance, and with the general consensus of the church fathers who unanimously assure us that the prophets also predicted these things which must be fulfilled many centuries later?
Answer: No.

Dubium III
Can one assume that the prophets, who not only reproved human wickedness and proclaimed the word of God for the benefit of their hearers, but also predicted future events, always necessarily had to speak not to men in the future but to contemporaries who were present in order to be able fully to be understood by them;

95

and that consequently the second part of the book of Isaiah (40–66), in which the seer does not address and offer comfort to men of Judah of Isaiah's time but Jews who are sorrowing in the Babylonian exile as though he lives among them, cannot have been written by Isaiah himself, who then was long since dead, but that it must be attributed to an unknown prophet who lived among the exiles?

Answer: No.

Dubium IV

Must one give such weight to the linguistic argument from word-usage and style, which serves to dispute the unity of the author of the book of Isaiah, that it compels a serious person, proficient in criticism and in the Hebrew language, to assume a multiple author-ship for that book?

Answer: No.

Dubium V

Are there solid arguments which, when one takes them together with each other, incontestably prove that the book of Isaiah must be attributed not to Isaiah alone but to two or even more authors?

Answer: No.

Roman Catholic biblical scholars felt that thereafter they had to keep the results of their investigations to themselves. For example, anyone asked to write about the development of messianic expecta-tions in the Old Testament found himself compelled to resort to tortuous explanations. After presenting Isaiah's view of the Messiah (approximately 740–700 BC), he would go on to that of Jeremiah (about 627–586) and then to that of Ezekiel (after 593). After that he had to discuss the view of the future which Isaiah (740–700) had sketched for the exiles in Babylon once Cyrus had appeared on the scene (after 550).

Catholics who wanted to write anything about the controversy over the 'servant of the Lord' who appears in Isaiah 42, 49, 50, 52, 53 and 61 had to express themselves in roughly the following way: '(According to the Biblical Commission) Isaiah experienced the time of the exile in the spirit, and he addresses the exiles of the future as though he were living among them. Thus in the interpretation of these chapters we can take into account the special circumstances of the exile which Isaiah had in view when he wrote them.'[65]

Instruction along these lines was given to priests in seminaries throughout the world. I well remember how, in 1937, we protested against the falsity of such instruction: 'Our professor himself does not believe what he is telling us.'

Things were different in the Dutch Reformed Church. They had no Papal Biblical Commission, and there was no apparatus for keeping a watchful eye on the seminaries. However, belief in divine inspiration served as an authority, and was all the stronger because it was not imposed externally. In his 1952 *Introduction*, mentioned above, Professor Aalders defended the authorship of Isaiah on traditional grounds. For him, these grounds included the references in the New Testament which are explicitly attributed to the prophet himself, and not merely to the book that bears his name. Of course, Aalders was familiar with all the arguments of modern criticism, but like the Papal Biblical Commission of 1908, he found them unconvincing. The narrative in chapters 36–39 could very well have been written by Isaiah himself. The appearance of all kinds of new ideas and conceptions in chapter 40 was still no indication of a new author. 'This is all the more convincing when a person in all seriousness takes into account the fact that here *we are not dealing merely with human concepts but with divine revelation*. There is no reason at all why God should not have imparted a different content of revelation to one and the same prophet at different periods of his prophetic activity.' The change in language and style proves nothing: 'A writer would have to have a very limited vocabulary indeed if he did not use terms and modes of expression in one case which he would refrain from using in other works.'

Finally, it is a characteristic of prophecy to describe the future as though it were already present. Isaiah could have anticipated in reality the destruction of Jerusalem and the exile which were to come about much later, and he could have known the name of the Persian ruler Cyrus at a time when his contemporaries were not even aware that Persia existed. 'But, some will say to us, is it likely that Isaiah would maintain over so many chapters that he had been transported into a distant future, describing it as though it were already present? The answer to this is that a phenomenon of this kind is indeed

97

unique: *but why should we claim the right to set limits to God's spirit?* Is this spirit not powerful enough to accomplish on a large scale with Isaiah what he had repeatedly done with other prophets on a smaller scale?'[66]

God can indeed do anything. He can permit someone to see and experience a situation of 150 years later, and can cause him to write words which fit this situation perfectly. But why should he?

On a first reading of Isaiah 40–55 we can see how the prophet is constantly in conversation with his audience, and how again and again he responds to their reactions. However, he cannot be a messenger from God who really lived among the exiles. This view is illegitimate, because of the dogma of the inspiration and the historical reliability of the Bible. In that case who is really placing limitations on the spirit of God?

3. Chronicles: history and 'fables'

In what period did people begin to think that a biblical story is true only when it is a faithful record of historical facts? We would need a specialist in cultural history to answer that question. However, it seems to me that this narrowing of the concept began only after the Middle Ages. In any case, it led to great difficulties after the emergence of historical criticism. Those engaged in this critical study showed that much of what is related in the scriptures cannot have happened in this way. Believers told them that they were misled by their prejudices: 'You think in your pride that God (even if you believe in his existence) cannot intervene in this world; so he can do no miracles and cannot reveal to men what will happen long after their own time; therefore you say that certain biblical stories cannot be true.' Believers who were better informed about things found such an answer inadequate. They knew that the Bible sometimes relates the same event in two very different ways. Both of these accounts cannot be true. Do we then have to accept that one of them is untrue? But that is impossible for anyone who accepts divine inspiration and with it the inerrancy of the Bible, the utter absence of any error. In that case, what is to be done with the conflicting reports?

I have chosen Chronicles as an example of a book of the Bible which more than once has put orthodox readers in this difficult position. The arrangement of the work is very simple:

I Chronicles	1–9	Genealogies (beginning with Adam)
	10–29	The reign of David
II Chronicles	1–9	The reign of Solomon
	10–36	The reigns of the kings of Judah

It appears from this arrangement that the writer is principally interested in David, his son Solomon, and all the successors in his dynasty down to the fall of Jerusalem. Now in the course of his narrative he cites all kinds of sources from which he has drawn his material. They are usually 'prophecies', 'visions', or 'books' which bear the name of a prophet; sometimes they are also a 'book of the kings of Judah' or a 'commentary (*midrash*) on the book of kings'. None of these documents has been preserved for us, unless the two books last mentioned are the biblical books of Samuel and Kings. It is certain that the writer of Chronicles had these books, or a version of them, before him when he wrote his own work. Any reader of the Bible can verify this for himself by comparing with Chronicles the corresponding texts in Samuel and Kings. But if he does that he will also encounter difficulties. Chronicles often gives quite a different version.

The best-known example is the story of the census which David made at God's command and for which he was punished by an epidemic among his people. He bought the threshing floor of Araunah, just outside Jerusalem, along with Araunah's oxen, for fifty shekels of silver. Once he had built an altar there, and sacrificed the oxen on it, God brought the plague to an end.

I Chronicles 21 repeats this story from II Samuel 24 with striking differences. Here it is Satan who prompts David to conduct the census. David sees the destroying angel with his drawn sword. He is more generous towards Araunah (here spelt Ornan) and gives him six hundred gold shekels. The sacrifice is consumed by a fire which comes from heaven.

In cases like this one can try to show that there are really no differences, by 'harmonizing' the texts. The expedient is to say that both accounts are dependent on an earlier account with far more detail, which one writer used in one way and one in another. Or one finds still other ways of eliminating the repugnant idea that there are discrepancies in scripture. God alone knows how much time, energy and ingenuity is devoted to this kind of effort to 'safeguard' the truth of the Bible.

In 1939, a German commentary on Chronicles by a Roman Catholic biblical scholar was published which came to be regarded as a norm for many years to come.[67] The author pointed out that the question of the historical reliability of Chronicles presents a special difficulty to 'Bible-believing interpreters, especially Roman Catholics, for whom the inerrancy of every historical work in the Bible is upheld as a matter of principle'. With overwhelming erudition which makes so many pages of this bulky volume almost unreadable the author bravely investigates all the historical difficulties; time and again, however, he has to concede that 'they cannot be solved at the moment'. In the case of the story of David's sacrifice, mentioned above, he takes refuge in the assumption that the two stories derive from a common source: the writer in II Samuel is supposed to have omitted the reference to the heavenly fire recorded in I Chronicles, as he 'preferred a less expressive description'.

The encyclical *Divino afflante* of 1943 also opened up the study of Chronicles for Roman Catholics. The Biblical Commission had not paid explicit attention to this book. It was, however, covered by the second 'answer' issued by the Commission in June 1905: it is wrong to assume too readily that biblical narratives which give the impression of presenting genuine history in fact set out to tell a parable or something of that kind, rather than retailing hard facts. Roman Catholic advocates of the inerrancy of the Bible had tried to adopt this approach. Shortly beforehand, the Commission had likewise blocked off another way out. Its first 'answer' dealt with 'implicit quotations'. Where the inspired writer tells an improbable story some would argue that without acknowledging the fact he was quoting a source of authority and did not accept responsibility for what he was saying. This was another way in which Catholic interpreters of the Bible had tried to preserve the doctrine of inspiration: in this way improbabilities and contradictions could be attributed to others besides the inspired writer himself. However, the Commission said that this approach was possible only when it could be demonstrated that the sacred writer was really quoting, and that he clearly dissociated himself from the source that he quoted.

All these tortuous devices were rendered superfluous in 1943. From then on Catholic interpreters could join other advocates of historical criticism with a clear conscience. In these circles, the assessment of Chronicles had undergone considerable changes since the time of Wellhausen. As a child of his time, Wellhausen had spoken brashly and scornfully about the author, the Chronicler, for whom religion seemed to consist entirely of the externals of the liturgy and who seemed to confine God within the strait-jacket of a strict doctrine of retribution. In order to prove his second-rate views, he seemed to have manipulated good historical documents without using any artistic skill. In other words, he was a tedious falsifer of history. More recent criticism on the one hand recognized the historical reliability of a number of details in Chronicles which were a valuable supplement to the tradition in Kings, and on the other hand began to appreciate the way in which the Chronicler had expressed the insights and expectations current in his milieu. This evaluation of Chronicles soon became common currency among Catholics, in part because it was expressed in translations of the Bible intended for ordinary church people. One of these translations says that the Chronicler sometimes hands down reliable historical material, but that there are times when he

gives facts at variance with the account offered by Samuel and Kings, or when he even deliberately modifies these accounts. This would be unforgivable in a historian of today whose job is to narrate and explain the sequence of events. But the author of Chronicles has no such intention. He is not a historian; he is a theologian. Contemplating the long history of Israel and particularly the Davidic episode, he paints a picture of the ideal kingdom. Past, present and future merge into one; into the age of David he projects the actual organization of his own, omits all that might diminish his hero, David, who for him is the type of the longed-for messianic king. Apart from certain fresh items of information, the value of which must be independently tested, the work is not so much a record of the past as a picture of the conditions and interests of the author's own period.[68]

Such an approach no longer has any difficulties with the 600 gold shekels which the Chronicler makes David pay for the threshing floor. According to experts on biblical monetary values, this is about 200 times the amount that David pays in II Samuel, i.e. fifty silver shekels. Here the Chronicler is thinking of the Temple, which was built on the site of the threshing floor, and for him David is the model of generosity when worship is involved. So the Chronicler makes him give an enormous amount of gold for the sacred plot, instead of buying it with silver. The amount becomes 600 gold shekels. For, once again contrary to the account in II Samuel, according to the Chronicler David is ruler over all twelve tribes from the very beginning: this leads him to multiply the number fifty in his source by twelve. Indeed, he believes that in the last resort it was God himself, rather than David, who destined the threshing floor to be the site of the Temple. He expresses this belief in ancient biblical terms, by means of the fire that falls from heaven, a miraculous bolt of lightning which consumes David's burnt offering, and which he also introduces at a later stage into the story of Solomon's dedication of the Temple.

This approach is still unacceptable to those who hold to the orthodox approach. Aalders, who is well aware of the new evaluation of Chronicles, makes this very clear: 'Such an evaluation of Chronicles is diametrically opposed to our point of departure, that the Old Testament, as part of the Bible, is the infallible word of God. In agreement with Article 4 of our Dutch Confession of Faith, we declare, "*We believe without doubt all that is contained in it.*" ' This forces him to use tortuous devices of the kind that we mentioned above. For example, he thinks that he can close the gap between the different amounts of money mentioned in the story of the threshing floor by envisaging the shekels in Chronicles as 'circular metal discs weighing very much less'.

Now it is true that anyone who rejects the principle that the biblical stories are completely accurate avoids a great many difficulties. However, that does not avoid others of a much more serious kind. One of them is connected with the scope of the Bible. Towards the end of the first century of the Christian era, the rabbis in Palestine restricted severely the number of recognized books in the biblical canon. They excluded a number of devotional writings which were, however, included in holy scripture by Jews who read their Bible in a Greek translation. Because the Christians read the Jewish Bible in the Greek version, they too included in it some writings which had been excluded by the Palestinian rabbis.

Among the church fathers, it was primarily the scholars who took these differences into account. Jerome lived in Bethlehem and took lessons from rabbis. Engaged in the task of translating the Bible into good Latin for the benefit of the Roman church, he felt some hesitation when the time came to deal with those books which according to his Jewish teachers were no part of holy scripture. Nevertheless, as he says in the preface to Tobit, in the end he submitted to the general feeling of the church rather than to the insights of the rabbis.

The Reformation was dominated by the theme of 'back to the sources', on which great stress was laid at the time. Its supporters would accept as books of the Old Testament only those writings which were also recognized among the Jews as the Bible. In this way it came to deny the inspired character of the others, which came to be called the Apocrypha. The synod of Dordrecht, which in 1618 decided to make a new translation of the Bible, did, however, hesitate to leave the Apocrypha out of the new *Statenbijbel* altogether. Had they done so, the Dutch churches would have parted company from the Anglican and Lutheran churches in neighbouring countries which had kept to the Bible in its older extent. It was therefore decided to make a place for the Apocrypha in an appendix, after the last book of the New Testament, with separate pagination, set in less attractive type, without marginal notes, and prefaced by a 'Warning to the reader'. This warning explained why the apocryphal books could not be held to be scripture. The most explicit proof was that they contained 'untrue, absurd, fabulous and contradictory matters' which were not in harmony with either the truth or the authentic books of the Bible.

Those who now accept that some stories in Chronicles are entirely or in part figments of a pious imagination must go on to ask whether in that case there is still reason for excluding such books as Tobit and Judith from the Bible. To give just one instance: the story in II Chronicles 20 is now seen as an expression of the belief that the strength and the salvation of the Jewish community are dependent on prayer and praise. After a moving prayer made by King Jehoshaphat, the representative of the people, and an exhortation by a prophet, the forces of Judah go out to meet the innumerable hosts of the three armies marching against them. In the front ranks march the Levites, clothed in their liturgical garments. As soon as they catch sight of the enemy, they begin to praise the Lord in a loud voice. The enemy armies immediately turn their weapons against one another, and all the Jews have to do is to carry away the spoil from among the corpses, a task that takes them three days. Anyone who recognizes that the primary aim of the Chronicler here is to portray the faith of his community and in so doing to strengthen it cannot go on objecting in principle to the claim to 'inspiration' of a work like the book of Judith.

4. The loss of the old certainties

Some time during 1963 a minister friend telephoned me. 'You're an expert in the spelling of old place names in the Bible; can you help me?' He had undertaken to translate a book describing archaeological excavation in the lands of the Bible. When I asked him what the book was he told me the title. It was in German, *Und die Bibel hat doch Recht* – the Bible was right after all (when the book was published in English it was simply called *The Bible as History*). I had never heard of it and got very cross: 'What a swindle! What a terrible title!' After some discussion I eventually promised to help on one condition, that he should see the Dutch edition was given another title. Of course I should have realized that as translator he could not possibly enforce such a condition. No publisher would want to give up such a winner!

But I was very angry indeed about the title. I had been involved in excavations in Palestine often enough to know what visitors expected by way of 'proofs' of the trustworthiness of the Bible. And I knew how journalists misused what we told them, and above all what we did not tell them, in order to pander to the wishes of their readers. So as soon as I heard the title I knew what kind of a book this was going to be: a collection of dated information, done up with the sauce of a fresh journalistic style, with the aim of comforting the dear believers in their uncertainty. They have heard from modern interpreters that the Bible is full of untruths. 'Now you can go back openly to what you always believed in your hearts but did not dare to express for fear of appearing old-fashioned. I shall prove from archaeology that the Bible is right after all . . .'

The book was translated into a number of languages and hundreds of thousands of copies were sold. In as far as biblical scholars took any notice of it, they criticized it severely. This shows how great the gulf still is between biblical scholars on the one hand and church people on the other. Things have not changed much since the situation identified by Lutz as early as 1840. In a Swiss theological journal of 1956 one can read something that sounds like an echo of Wellhausen's complaint of 1842: 'in fact I am making my hearers unfit for a ministry in the church.' The more recent article is talking about a minister who cannot accept the historicity of the biblical stories about Abraham.

> In view of his responsibility to his congregation and to the church, he will only be able to declare his convictions openly with pain and fear. For quite apart from the fact that he will be raising grave doubts among the flock entrusted to him and will not be giving them the firm support in life that they need, he will be conscious that he is laying open the form and content of the whole Bible to a process of erosion once he denies the historicity – and with it the truth – of such an important part of it. A theologian with a sense of responsibility, whose intellectual integrity leads him to accept such a conclusion, can at best find a way out of his dilemma by trying to avoid the Abraham stories as far as possible. We know pastors who never preach about Abraham and never use his history when teaching the faith.[69]

As a conclusion to this chapter, I shall try to list some of the questions and doubts raised by the historical approach, beginning with the Old Testament. I shall do this briefly and concisely, without bothering too much about finer distinctions.

Thanks to excavations and textual studies, our knowledge of the world in which ancient Israel lived has increased greatly since the end of the last century. However, the specific figures of the patriarchs of Israel are still veiled in darkness. According to the best experts on this period of the history of the near East, they will always remain so, because of the character of the biblical narratives. This holds true for Moses and the exodus, and equally for the early history of the Israelite tribes in Canaan.

We have seen how sharply those who held a traditional belief about the Bible reacted to the new approach, especially when Wellhausen presented it so convincingly. They felt that he put the whole doctrine of inspiration in doubt, and with it the whole of Christian faith. This feeling grew even stronger when people in the church later began to lay stress on 'the historical character of revelation'. God reveals himself, it was said, in and through facts. The terms 'salvation history' and 'saving facts' began to be used everywhere. So the old question was posed in a new form: what kind of revelation comes to us in facts of which we do not know the true nature? The promise to Abraham, Moses, the exodus, the revelation on Sinai, the conquest of the promised land are all supposedly fundamental facts of salvation, and yet the scholars say that nothing can be said with any certainty about any of them.

One possibility, of course, is to accuse the scholars of fostering doubt and in spite of them to maintain the 'historical nucleus' in these saving facts. Another is to say that it is not the facts themselves which are revelatory, but the stories about them which Israel told and wrote down. In that case it is the faith of Israel which is 're-velatory', and what actually happened does not become an issue. But in that case, what becomes of the God who works in history?

Yet another difficulty seemed to be no less serious. The historical approach included an attempt to understand the ancient texts in terms of their own time. They were so to speak restored to their original setting. The question put to the text was always, what did the man who wrote this down mean to say at the time? Such an approach posed the problem: what use is a book from before the time of Christ to men of the modern world? After all, in Christ all previous revelation came to a climax which was never to be surpassed thereafter. Why then continue to drag along this ballast from an incomplete pre-history?

In the second century of our era, the scholar Marcion proposed to the churches that they should drop the Old Testament entirely and retain of the New only those parts which bore witness to the 'strange' God of love who had been made manifest in Jesus. When modern criticism had restored the ancient biblical texts to their original setting, the very same proposal was made by a great German scholar. Wellhausen and other kindred spirits had, without saying as much openly, studied the Old Testament as the document of an ancient religion in very much the same way as other scholars analysed the texts of other ancient religions. In 1920, in a large-scale study of Marcion, the German scholar to whom I am referring, Adolf von Harnack, wrote that for the Protestant churches to keep the Old Testament at the present time could only be seen as the consequence of a religious and ecclesiastical paralysis.[70]

So the Nazis found support among Christian theologians when, in their hatred for all that was Jewish, they tried to ban the Old Testament as a product of 'the inferior Jewish mind'. Other Christians reacted promptly. In 1934, a book by Wilhelm Vischer was published with the expressive title *The Witness of the Old Testament to Christ*. According to this interpretation, the age-old interpretation of Christianity, the imperishable value of the Old Testament, lay in the witness it bore to Christ. But how did it bear that witness? Following the church fathers, all succeeding generations had assumed that the Spirit had given the texts of the Old Testament inspired meanings which were hidden from the Jews, but had now been made clear to the members of Christ's church. However, this way of reading them had become impossible for modern Christians. This had happened predominantly because they could no longer believe in such a form of inspiration, with the result that the interpretations made by the church fathers seemed to be quite arbitrary patchwork. Answers to this particular problem are still being sought. The great Rudolf Bultmann proposed that the Old Testament should be seen as the history of a failure. He pointed out that all efforts to realize a right relationship to God within an earthly community come to nothing. So the Old Testament is 'prophecy' by virtue of its own inner contradiction, and reading the ancient book can show the Christian paths that he must not take. According to Bultmann, the same lesson can also be learnt from secular texts and from encounters and incidents in personal experience. However, other theologians have found this approach too negative. But they have yet to find an unequivocal answer to give to the question of the role that the Old Testament should play in the Christian church.[71]

'What becomes of the New Testament if people begin to apply such theories to the gospels as well?' I was surprised to read this sentence in the conclusion to a short book written by the Jesuit scholar Leopold Fonck and published in Innsbruck in 1905.[72] According to the title, he set out to describe 'the battle over the truth of holy scripture in the past twenty-five years'. Was he not aware that the phenomenon about which he was writing had already been in process for almost a century? Or was he talking about its penetration into 'the Roman Catholic camp'? In any case, his book says nothing about Reimarus, whose writings were edited for publication by the great Lessing, beginning in 1794. These writings marked the start in Germany of the 'quest for the historical Jesus', which was to be pursued with such passion. If, after the Enlightenment, it was no longer possible to believe in supernatural factors like revelation or the inspiration of the Bible, or in dogmas like the incarnation, what could really be said about the life of Jesus and what significance did it still have for modern men? In 1902, an account of the 'quest of the historical Jesus' was published. The author was Albert Schweitzer, and it covered the period from Reimarus to the biblical scholar William Wrede, whose book on *The Messianic Secret in the Gospel of Mark* had appeared the previous year. While Schweitzer went his own way, Wrede later became one of the pioneers of the method of 'form criticism'. From the 1920s onwards, this approach to the gospels began to dominate research. Like Moses, now Jesus too, his person and his work, seemed to disappear in the mists of uncertainty; the new scientific study of the gospels showed that they bear witness only to the faith of the early church, and that it was no longer possible to go back behind their testimony to the historical existence of Jesus.

In 1966 these uncertainties led to a sharp conflict in Germany. Orthodox church leaders called for a protest. Whereas earlier there had been talk of a steadily widening gap between biblical scholars and those with orthodox views of the Bible, the signs now pointed to a 'gaping abyss'. It no longer seemed possible to bridge the gulf.

On 6 March 1966, with the sound of a thousand trumpets, the battle commenced. It was a battle between the congregations of the church and professors engaged in biblical criticism, a battle over Jesus, his words and his miracles, over belief in the virgin birth and the resurrection. 22,000 Protestants filled the Westfalenhalle in Dortmund for a great rally which proved to be a combination of heresy trial and prayer meeting.

The issue was sensational enough for the editor of the weekly journal *Der Spiegel* to devote special attention to it.[73] He published a series of articles stressing the numerous differences of opinion among leading German theologians over the most important points of belief in Jesus. The last article had a very journalistic ending. The writer quoted a sentence from Luther which refers to Jesus' promise that he would be with his disciples until the end of the world. Then he quoted a similar confession of faith by a modern theologian: 'It is he, Jesus, who preserves the church.' The concluding line which the writer added consisted of only two words: 'Which Jesus?'

There is, of course, one way of avoiding all these uncertainties. People unite in groups from which the new approach is carefully excluded. 'We hold fast to the confession and we believe without any doubt everything that is written in holy scripture.' In Holland this has led to separation, and then to further separation from the separated group. Shortly after the war I visited an Old Testament professor in Kampen. It did not surprise me that he argued vigorously in favour of Moses' authorship of the Pentateuch. A shiver did, however, run down my spine when he showed me a pamphlet which he had written himself and which identified the synodal church, from which his group had separated, with the great harlot of the book of Revelation. There was something gruesome about the certainty of the belief of his small group that it was the only true church of Christ, excluding all others throughout the entire world. We have already come across Henri Poels, the priest who suffered for his views on the Pentateuch. In 1898, he had written, in a style common at the time, about

the little mother who always sits at the same window with her knitting. For her this one street is the whole world. She has never seen the Alps. For her there is nothing higher than the spires in her little village. This dear soul thinks that the great clock at which she is looking, through lace curtains that are always drawn, tells the time for all mankind under God's sun. And our little mother does not sit knitting alone. People intelligent enough to remove churches are peering through the same window.

Poels was writing for Catholics who did not want to hear of a new approach. Even in a world-wide church like the Catholic church, the retention of old certainties can be a sign of narrowness of mind and spirit.

The most extreme example of this is provided by Jehovah's Witnesses, who are represented in almost every country in the world. Members must believe in the inspiration of the Bible in the strictest sense of the word. Along with this goes a system of 'interpretation' which is equally binding and is officially prescribed for all groups, all over the world, by the central authority. To ask critical questions is to be affected by 'the spirit of the evil world'. To become a Jehovah's Witness marks the beginning of a process in which all links with the world are broken. The conclusion is a reasonable one. For them it is true that anyone who raises questions or admits doubts can no longer bear witness.

III · From an Impasse to the Whole World

It looks as though there are only two ways out of the impasse. One is to hold fast to the old doctrine of inspiration and thus to the divine authority of the Bible. In that case we remain faithful to the old formulations, the confessions and doctrinal statements of the church which express this belief and are based on it. And in our thinking about the Bible we simply refuse to admit any human views which might seem to attack these certainties. This is the way of well-defined doctrine, with a clear distinction between belief and unbelief. It is also the way adopted by any clearly-defined group, church, or – if you like to call it that – sect.

Alternatively, we may endorse the historical approach without any reservation. That means analysing the Bible as though it were any other ancient book, with the appropriate critical methods. In that case we see any supernatural events, 'acts of God', miracles, prophecies, in it as expressions of the faith of a people who had a different world view from our own. And in that case the Bible contains no objective divine revelation. In itself, it is no more authoritative than any other religious book. This approach is one of unrestrained modernism. Subjective opinions take the place of objective truths. It is no longer possible to point to common ground on which a group, church or sect might be founded. This way inevitably leads to the dissolution of the existing churches and ultimately of Christianity.

In this chapter I want to argue for a third possibility, a kind of middle way which seems to be being taken by more and more Christians. They have unreservedly opted for the historical approach, but they combine with this an attitude which they feel can quite legitimately be called faith. In their view this way leads to a new shared appreciation and experience of what the Bible is really about.

In such a short book I can do no more than sketch out what such an approach entails. I shall begin with a few remarks the significance of which may only emerge a little later on.

1. A new climate

The atmosphere when the Society for Biblical Literature and Exegesis met in New York at the end of December 1964 was more festive than usual. This was the hundredth meeting since the founding of the Society in 1880. The book containing the papers given on that occasion demonstrates its ecumenical character. Scholars joined in from many countries, and from Protestant, Roman Catholic and Jewish circles. 'Perhaps the most amazing conclusion to which some reader will come is that the agreements among writers outnumber their disagreements.'[74]

No biblical scholar will be surprised at this. He takes it for granted that he has to keep up with the research done by his colleagues in his field, by going to meetings and congresses when he has time and money for them, and always by reading the scholarly journals. When it comes to biblical scholarship, it is usually difficult to tell from which church or denomination a writer comes. That is unimportant; the important thing is the strength of his arguments. Of course, to study the meaning of ancient texts is not like mathematics. There is nothing here like the certainty of mathematical proofs. Biblical criticism is a historical study; the force of an argument can depend in part on a capacity to understand the material sympathetically, on deeply rooted preconceptions and so on, which may be conditioned by temperament and education, and even by a particular church background. However, in genuine discussion all these factors can be freely acknowledged and discussed.

In short: *the discipline of biblical scholarship brings together people from various nations and churches in a spirit of objective research.* This also means that, when necessary, they can begin to take a more historical approach to the claims of their own church or confession.

One example may help to make this clear. In Matthew 16, Jesus says, 'You are Peter, and on this rock I will build my church.' Since the Reformation there has been a good deal of argument as to what this saying means. In the past, though, it was never doubted that Jesus had spoken these words on a particular day in the vicinity of Caesarea Philippi. The inter-confessional argument sometimes took on the character of a 'Yes it is – no it isn't' quarrel, in which everyone decided what the text must or must not mean from the perspective of his own thought-world.

That kind of approach has now become impossible. A historical approach begins with the person who wrote the text. Here it was the author of the First Gospel, identified by the name Matthew. The style of writing and the terminology of this author is analysed, and so is the way in which he arranged the material that he had at his disposal. Did that material include the Gospel of Mark? It looks as though Matthew has inserted Jesus' promise into Mark's narrative as an answer to Peter's confession. Matthew wants to make this confession clearer by adding 'the Son of the living God'. Why did Matthew do this at just this point? The word *ecclesia*, meaning church or community, appears only on one occasion outside this passage in the four gospels, and that is in Matthew 18; there it appears in a saying of Jesus which is very much in Matthew's style. Did Jesus in fact talk about his future *ecclesia*? If so, must that not have been just before his passion, or after his resurrection? And what did he have in mind when he did so?

These are far from being the only questions raised by the text. It seems to me unlikely that those involved in studying it ever think about the papacy, whether for or against. As far as they are concerned, that lies in an entirely different dimension, even if they are unaware that it was in fact centuries before the text came to be used in connection with this specific issue (as we have already seen, even Augustine did not seem aware of such a use).

To take another example: since the Reformation, people have tended to understand Paul in terms of the personal struggles of Luther, which were very closely connected with the experience of faith in his time. People began to make Paul say all sorts of things about sin, law and grace which he did not intend and could not have meant. Preoccupation with one's conscience became customary only some centuries after Paul, and then in the western part of the church. This recognition can provide a new vision of what Paul did

113

mean, and also help us, for example, to see whether 'justification by faith' really does lie at the heart of the gospel. It is encouraging that a Scandinavian scholar from the Lutheran church should have been the one who pointed to the influence of Luther and his time on the interpretation of Paul, during a discussion between Catholics and Protestants held some years ago at Harvard.[75]

Biblical research along these lines can also help towards another piece of ecumenical understanding. It shows that *the Bible does not proclaim a doctrine, in the sense of a structured set of doctrinal propositions.*

Jesus did not give any new teaching in this sense. We saw that in the first chapter of this book. Where the New Testament tries to express the significance of Christ's person and work, it seems that each writer follows his own line of thought, influenced to a greater or lesser degree by the thought patterns current in his environment. So it cannot be said that the New Testament gives us one particular doctrine about Christ, a 'christology'. It has almost become a truism to say that in the New Testament several christologies can be found in juxtaposition, which cannot be reduced to any common denominator without doing violence to the thinkers and writers of the early church. There was a variety in the experience and confessions of the early church which in later centuries was all too often forgotten. Anyone who claims that the New Testament is binding on the church must accept and encourage such variety.

The same is true of the Old Testament. It is often suggested that this collection of books is dominated by one and the same view of Israel's history, 'salvation history'. B. van Iersel recently pointed to the many variations in the survey of salvation history offered in the Bible. He concluded:

> Because of these many variations one cannot, in my view, speak of *the* history of salvation. Which to my mind suggests that in fact there is no such thing. What we have is histories of salvation, in the plural. And there are many of these. The specific forms of these salvation histories are closely connected, on the one hand with the literary context in which they appear, and on the other with the historical situation in which they function.[76]

Furthermore, there are entire books which appear to know nothing

114

of such salvation history. In Proverbs, Job and Ecclesiastes the names of Israel and Jerusalem do not appear, nor do the concepts of covenant and election. Alongside the ecstatic jubilation of believers who see God as overwhelmingly active in particular facts, to which testimony is given in so many hymns in the book of Psalms and in the prophetic writings, there are utterances by people who cannot discover any way at all in which God is active in history. One might think of Ecclesiastes, the preacher, and perhaps even more of Agur, the wise man in Proverbs 30. According to some translators, the remarks of this man are supposed to mean that he had become weary in his search for the meaning of things. But there is much to indicate that the utterance of Agur originally was, 'There is no God, there is no God, and I am exhausted.' We can well understand how this would be too strong for the ancient copyists and translators of the text.[77]

This brings me to my third preliminary comment. One feels that *many Christians in our time are reluctant to use the word 'God'*. This could be connected with, and conducive of, an understanding and use of the Bible which is *less self-assured*.

It is as difficult for people to talk about God now as it was easy for them to do so earlier. Some find themselves embarrassed or perplexed when they hear others speaking about God as though they were referring to a well-known entity, clearly defined, which could be brought into conversation and reasoning at will. Resistance to this use of the word God is not lessened when the Bible is cited in this connection. On the contrary, anyone who talks fluently about God in biblical terms can count on antipathy from an increasing number of people: 'God has said this or that; God usually does this or that; look at the ways of God; we admire and praise his mighty acts which are recorded in his Word which we have here in our hands, this book, God's Word . . .'

Why is there increasing resistance to such talk? Perhaps a growing number of people are more concerned than ever before that innumerable human beings are oppressed, ill-treated and killed in the name of this clearly defined biblical God. Charlemagne, who had thousands of Saxons killed because of their unbelief in this God, was not the first to do so, nor, alas, are the soldiers of the Wehrmacht, who had *Gott mit uns* on their belt-buckles, likely to be the last.

People do not know how to cope with the idea of a God who allows himself to be put at the disposal of force and tyranny.

Be this as it may, a degree of reserve in talking about God seems to be a help in coming in contact with the people who are talking to us in the biblical texts. The theme is regularly expressed in the Old Testament: anyone who has caught a glimpse of God must die. In this way those who appear in the Bible express the idea that God is so overwhelmingly different from man that in any genuine encounter with him man would die. There was a realization that some people had been granted a privilege which was referred to as 'walking with God'. Of these, the most favoured was Moses, with whom, according to Exodus 33, God spoke 'face to face, as a man speaks with his fellow man'. Later in the same chapter, however, it is related that God said to Moses, 'You cannot see my face, for no man can see my face and live.'

Paul tells the Corinthians, who were so concerned to obtain deep insights, that a sure knowledge of God is granted to us in faith: this knowledge, however, is only partial, and to talk on the basis of it, however prophetic that may be, is only childish prattle.

At present, there is growing interest in the great figures who have had experience of God, whom we call mystics. Each, in his or her own way, bears witness to the absolute otherness of God, who can be known only in the darkness of faith. The very greatest of those who 'talk about God', whom we call theologians, confirm this. In Thomas Aquinas we find sayings like: 'The better we come to know God in this life, the better we comprehend that he is above all that can be grasped by the understanding.' When Thomas Aquinas was seized by a fatal illness in 1274, on his way to a council, he was reading the Song of Solomon, that favourite book of Christian mystics since Origen.

Even if there were no other considerations, more profound awareness of the nature of the mystery of existence that we call 'God' will make it harder and harder for Christians to withdraw into closed groups. They will no longer be able to claim that 'We possess the truth', 'The pure faith is to be found only with us.'

2. Israel: God creates a community

What we have called the 'historical approach' in earlier chapters might also be termed 'taking a detached view'. The biblical scholars of the last century detached themselves from a pattern of church life in which the Bible held a central position. In faith, the Bible was seen and experienced as the word through which God time and again addresses man in a particular present. By dissociating themselves from that view, biblical scholars created the possibility of comparing the religion of ancient Israel with that of surrounding nations. In this way, the distinctive character of Israel's religion could come into focus.

In one of his sensitive short books, Romano Guardini once described how one might conceive the situation in which, according to the experts, the phenomenon of religion has its origin. They call it 'the religious experience'. In his account, Guardini tells of the experience of a friend:

He was walking alone through a forest and came to an open place. It was mid-day, and everything was filled with the profound quietness that can prevail at that hour. It was utterly still. No birds sang; nothing was moving. The tranquil warmth of the sun filled the area. Suddenly, he said, he was seized with a profound uneasiness. It was not fright, such as can be caused by something in particular, for example by an animal or by the feeling that another person is present, but something entirely different without any obvious cause, inexpressible, but so irresistible and overpowering that he ran away blindly, until he finally stopped, utterly exhausted and trembling all over. The narrator had experienced what the Greeks called the fear of Pan, 'panic'.

Now let us just imagine that this had not happened in our twentieth century, but in the seventh or eighth century before Christ; and not in a wooded area maintained by experienced foresters, but in a lonely primaeval forest of Asia Minor or northern Greece, and that the narrator himself was not a scientifically educated man of our time, but a herdsman who lived with his flock; and that he had something of what can be called religious genius, visionary power, the capacity to experience religious mystery and to express it in forms. In that case he might have seen a strange being sitting

117

on a boulder: half man and half animal, with terrifying eyes and pointed ears, and a powerful force could have emanated from this being, terror and attraction at the same time, both fascination and fear. Then this herdsman would have run to his comrades and said, 'A god has appeared to me!' And they would have called him Pan, the god of nature that is both familiar and alien, both alluring and terrifying.

We can imagine the rise of the conceptions of the gods as occurring in something like this fashion. People of an earlier time, who did not have a critical attitude towards things of life, but were directly open to them, experienced the mystery that is revealed in the world immediately around them and that yet led further, deeper, that bestows upon the world a special significance and at the same time causes it to be wrapped up in the ineffable. Moreover they had the ability to see it, not abstractly, but in images; in this way it was enacted for them in figures and happenings.[78]

After this, Guardini describes how the great realities in nature, such as sun, earth, sea and wind, become gods, figures whose actions and destinies are related in the kind of stories we call myths.

Something of this sort must also lie at the beginning of Israel's religion: an overpowering experience of the mystery that lies behind things, and a story in which that divine reality appears in action. The Bible has preserved only later formulations of all this. Starting from that recognition, we might perhaps say that the founders of Israel's religion must have experienced the mystery of existence more strongly than others as a Someone. The attractive aspect of this experience must then have consisted in the fact that the mystery which had a personal aspect disclosed itself as a saving, life-giving mystery. The aspect evoking fear then came to be expressed in the absoluteness and the inexorable character of its claims. Equally characteristic, however, was the fact that it did not 'claim' those who encountered it as separate individuals, but with an eye to their group. Thus it was a religious experience in which the mystery of existence was overwhelmingly presented as 'personality', seeking relationship and founding a community.

There was also a story connected with this experience. However,

118

the mystery did not appear in it in concrete form. This 'personality' was denoted by a name, by the four consonants YHWH. Nothing can be said at present with any certainty about the origin and meaning of this name. The ancient Israelites used it very freely. But in the last centuries before Christ the Jews began to avoid it. Where it appeared in the sacred texts they pronounced another word, 'the Lord', and when speaking or writing they tended to use paraphrases, like 'heaven', 'the name', 'the power', 'the dwelling' (in the Temple) and so on. It was probably pronounced Yahweh, but that is not certain. In his famous German translation of the Bible, Martin Buber aptly chose the personal pronoun as his rendering of YHWH. We might compare the following quotation from the psalms, which I have picked at random, with Buber's version:

> Sing to *the Lord* a new song . . .
> It is good to praise *the Lord* . . .
> How great are thy works, *O Lord*!

> Sing to *him* a new song . . .
> It is good to give thanks to *thee* . . .
> How great are thy deeds, *thou*!

The story is not enacted either wholly or in part in higher spheres, in a supra-terrestrial, divine world, but entirely on this earth. A group of slaves had made an effort to escape from Egypt. At a critical moment they had escaped the danger of total annihilation. 'He' had done this. In this way he had made this group his own people. Israel knew that it existed by the grace of his saving action. It would not even be there had he not intervened, in pure compassion for an oppressed people. So it kept repeating, in praise and prayer, his name, his own name, written out in full: 'He who led us out of Egypt'.

In this way the foundation was laid for *a religion which stands out from all others because of its attention to man*. The divine took shape, 'revealed itself', in a rescue from the inhuman condition of slavery and the creation of a society on the basis of a number of 'human rights', unequivocally formulated as absolute demands, demands from God. I am talking about the ancient formula which we call the ten commandments. It was suggested long ago that the commandments are intended as two sets of five, so that the Israelite could

119

count the fundamental truths of his faith on the fingers of both hands. I do not know who made the suggestion, but it is an illuminating one.

When God has introduced himself to his people, 'I am Yahweh who led you out of Egypt', he sums up his claims. The Israelite is not to acknowledge any power other than him. He must not make any image and in so doing suggest to himself or others that he has Yahweh at his disposal. That would also be the implication were he to use Yahweh's sacred name in pagan fashion as an instrument of magic. He must dedicate one day of the week, the sabbath, to Yahweh; this is to acknowledge that in fact all time, and thus the whole of creation, belongs to God. On the sabbath he is to ensure rest for himself and his fellow men, rest from the hard work that is a reminder of the killing slave labour of Egypt. Finally, he is to honour his parents, through whom Yahweh gave him life. For parents are not ordinary fellow men: they belong to the divine order.

Fellow men are the subject of the last five commandments, 'Do not kill', and so on. We should remember that 'kill' in this context does not mean killing in war or the death penalty as the outcome of a judicial process, but wilful murder; that 'steal' probably refers only to the kidnapping of a fellow man in order to make him a slave; and finally that 'covet' in ancient Hebrew in fact includes the actual seizure of something. Given this, it seems that Yahweh puts five fundamental human rights alongside his own claims: the rights of life, marriage, liberty, a good name and possessions. The rights of God and the rights of one's fellow men could then be counted off on the fingers of two hands, and these two hands can be joined in prayer.

In texts like Leviticus 19 we can see how the real reason for doing right to a fellow man, and more than that, is rooted in the person of Yahweh. Rules for society are interrupted time and again by the statement, 'I am Yahweh'. He has made himself known as the one who delivers men from distress, and by this saving act has called his people Israel into life. So the Israelite is as it were sinning against existence itself whenever he causes distress to another.

Thus another characteristic of the earliest literature of Israel is a great interest, exceptional in the ancient world, in what we call 'the phenomenon of man'. This appears specifically in the masterpiece that modern scholars call the 'succession narrative'. This describes how of all David's children Solomon at last becomes his successor, as the outcome of a series of human dramas which are described with an equal amount of sympathy and literary skill.

This concern for man is even more explicit in the great historical work that is customarily attributed to the 'Yahwist'.[79] We have seen how Wellhausen recognized this work as the foundation of the Pentateuchal narrative. Many contemporary scholars put the work in the reign of Solomon (about 970–930 BC) rather than in 850, i.e. before the disintegration of David's kingdom. We might perhaps summarize what this writer wants to say to his audience in the following way. 'The great kingdom of David in which you now belong and in which so many nations have been incorporated is not to be taken for granted and is not the last word. I have collected together all kinds of ancient sagas from the time before the state came into being to show you how our God Yahweh prepared for this great kingdom. But this gathering together of so many peoples in the kingdom of Yahweh is not the last word. His ultimate intention is for it to include all nations, and to cause them to share in the blessing which he bestowed upon Abraham. For he is concerned with mankind as a whole, *adam*. The first part of my story is meant to show you this. Yahweh created man and wanted him to be one family. But man refused to recognize Yahweh's divine sovereignty. The result was the oppression of brother by brother. Cain murdered his brother, and Lamech took seventy-seven fold revenge. The sorry story of a humanity that no longer acknowledges its Lord ends in the drama of the tower of Babel: the humanity that is meant to be God's family is broken apart, fragmented into numerous nations who no longer understand one another. You must see the calling of Abraham, and with it your own task in the history of mankind, against this background.'

During the following centuries we see the basic features of Israelite religion expressed primarily in the preaching of the prophets. Whereas people are born everywhere and at all times with what we would call a particular religious sensitivity, in Israel such gifted people naturally became 'prophets'. They felt themselves to be called, and they called others. For their experience of the divine could not be anything but an experience of Yahweh, at least when they grew up in a setting where the old tradition was alive. In that case, this experience naturally acquired the character of a 'calling'. For people saw the experience of Yahweh as a summons to fellowship, 'covenant': all the traditional stories, rites and institutions within the tradition stood under the sign of the covenant. So it is that by virtue of the very fact that they were seized by a strong sense of his presence, the prophets were aware of being 'sent' to their people, to restore fellowship according to God's original design: fellowship between Israel and Yahweh, and fellowship among men. That is why the prophetic preaching which has been handed down to us is dominated by the two great themes of the ten commandments. It protests against the recognition of other powers than Yahweh, or against idolatry, any tendency or effort to look for salvation to any other earthly or heavenly agency. In the name of this same Yahweh, it also protests against every form of injustice and oppression. Of course, the emphasis varies with each prophet, depending on his temperament and the situation with which he had to deal. Let me give a few examples.

In about 840 BC, in the northern kingdom, we see Elijah taking a stand for the rights of God and man. He represents circles in which the Yahwistic faith was experienced in its original purity. In agricultural Israel, people had begun to believe that rain and fertility must come from the local Baals, as the Canaanite population had always supposed. The king encouraged them in this view. To further trading relationships, King Ahab had married a princess from the Canaanite city of Tyre, and of course her Baal also had a temple of his own. According to Elijah, Israel was 'limping', by acknowledging other powers alongside Yahweh. He fought furiously for Yahweh's exclusive rights. So he took a firm stand against Ahab and his wife when she violated property rights and had an Israelite, Naboth, murdered so that she could add his vineyard to her own land.

While we know Elijah and his successor Elisha only from the stories which are told about them, powerful and dramatic though they are, we have first-hand knowledge of a prophet from the following century. A number of sayings of the prophet Hosea have come down to us. Round about 750 BC, this Hosea had to deal with an Israel which thought that it had to give thanks for the produce of the land, grain and flax, oil and wine, to the local Baals. He thought of

Israel as a woman, and the Baals as her lovers. By acting as she did, according to Hosea, Israel was offending against the love of Yahweh, her first and only Baal, that is, her husband and lord. Now he would have to bring down disaster upon her, and devastate her land, in order to bring her back, through this wilderness, to her first love. In this way Hosea depicts the nature of the one who, on his own initiative, delivered people from Egypt to make them his own, dedicated only to him. Particularly memorable are Hosea's sublime words about Yahweh as a passionate and jealous lover, as a father who cannot give up his ungrateful and rebellious son because his love is a divine love which, in degree though not in kind, transcends all human expressions of it. Israel is called to respond with what Hosea calls 'knowledge of God'. Whenever this is lacking, the land is dominated by all the forces which destroy human society: 'There is swearing, lying, killing, stealing and committing adultery; they break all bounds and murder follows murder.'[80] Hence his passionate reproach to the political and religious leaders who allow and perpetuate all this wickedness.

Some sayings from Hosea's contemporary Amos have also come down to us. He apparently lived in a village in the kingdom of Judah, and grew up in the ancient traditions of Yahwism. From there he travelled to the northern kingdom, which had taken over the ancient hallowed name of Israel. That kingdom did not, however, live up to its name. For Amos had heard that although the nation was prosperous, people in it were being exploited and trampled under foot. That was incompatible with the name Israel. Amos went straight to the source of all that evil, the royal Temple where the king and the priests came together. In the Temple, people revelled in the view of history prompted by their faith, and celebrated the constancy of Yahweh and the promises that he would not break: indeed, he would give still more blessings, more prosperity, even clearer signs of his favouritism towards Israel.

That was the target against which Amos directed his attack, with a savageness which constantly amazes the reader. All right, Israel had been chosen by Yahweh. But that meant that Israel had a greater responsibility than other nations, and would be severely punished for every form of injustice. Did the Israelites think that they were more important than others? The black people of Africa were just as precious to Yahweh. Did the exodus from Egypt make a difference? But had not Yahweh had a hand in all the great migrations? 'I also led the Philistines from Caphtor and the Syrians from Kir.' So Amos sees Yahweh as the God of all nations, and primarily as the universal protector of human rights. When these rights are infringed among his own people, he will relentlessly destroy that people. Perhaps he will spare something from the nation, but this remnant may well be rather like a sheep's ear, say, proof for the shepherd to show the owner of the flock that the animal was mangled by a wild beast.[81]

Shortly after the time of Amos, the great Isaiah took a stand for the rights of God and man. It looks as though those who compiled the book which contains his sayings wanted to keep the reader in suspense. First come several chapters with complaints and threats against the rulers and the people of Judah, who are boldly labelled, in the style of Amos, princes of Sodom and people of Gomorrah. Isaiah could hardly have thought of any epithets that would have been more offensive in that setting. In Judah, too, all kinds of injustices were being practised at the time. Rich men were seizing the houses and fields of the poor in order to have a monopoly of property owning. For that reason Yahweh loathed their religious observances in the Temple, with sacrifices, praise and incense. As earlier in Egypt, now again the anguished cries of the oppressed would move him to intervene and to strike a blow for his people. The destroying armies of Assyria were already on the march.

At this point, in chapter 6, the compilers of the book made Isaiah himself relate his call. At a time when the king of Assyria was preparing to take over sole rule of the entire world, in the year in which the king of David's line in Jerusalem died, Isaiah saw *the* king, Yahweh of hosts, on his heavenly throne. The significance of this vision has been well described by Fr Renckens. After describing the new significance which the expression 'Yahweh of hosts' had acquired, that of world God and creator God, he writes:

That world-wide character is shown to Isaiah in this vision. So the vision, put in positive terms, says that Yahweh is the God of the world and is beginning to reveal himself as God of the world. In other words, what he was for Israel alone up to this time, he will be, in the future, for the entire world and for all mankind. Put in negative terms, it says that the time of Israel's privileges as a nation is past. Israel has had its chance and did not use it, so Yahweh is turning away from Israel and will undertake on a world-wide scale what he did not succeed in achieving in Israel.

Isaiah encounters the ancient Yahweh of hosts, but now he is the God of the universe; the ancient Adonai, the national Master, but now the Lord Almighty. He is in the Temple in Jerusalem, but this place has cosmic dimensions; he is seated upon the ancient throne of the ark, but this has become the heavenly throne. He is the ancient Holy One of Israel, but now the thrice-holy God of the world, whose holiness is revealed in Israel in the cloud of glory, but whose glory now fills the whole earth. The ancient cherubim, with their limited task of bearing the throne and guarding the gates, are in Isaiah's vision ennobled and spiritualized into seraphim. The ultimate aim of all God's work is the revelation of his holiness. Yahweh's name must be hallowed on earth as it is in heaven, so that the earth too may be full of his glory. That ultimate aim in all its completeness is in God's view from all eternity; it is the inexhaustible subject of the celestial liturgy. And for one moment Isaiah is the privileged witness of it.

That makes all the more painful his awareness that he is a man standing in the midst of history, which as yet is only in the process of development towards that goal. The earth is still far from being full of Yahweh's glory, and the very nation in whose midst the king of glory dwells from of old is a sinful nation, a people of Sodom. That is his own people.

So this vision brings about a great change in Isaiah's thinking: Yahweh's salvation is destined for a new world-wide Israel, and conversely, it will bring great disaster on the old nationalistic Israel. The nation is hopelessly lost, but Isaiah still speaks to it. That is because it is brought home to him that a person of good will can be purified, even though it be by fire. The national catastrophe will be the purification and the salvation of many. So Yahweh speaks through Isaiah in order to form within his rejected nation, by means of his creative word, a remnant out of which the new Israel can grow, as though from a holy seed.[82]

This remnant is to consist of believers, in the sense in which Isaiah understands this term. They rely on Yahweh alone, and so they form a community which has as its motto Immanuel, 'God with us'. That is also the name of the one who represents this group, the one who will take the place of the unbelieving king Ahaz. Isaiah gives him grandiose names, but he does not call him king. That title belongs to Yahweh alone. Filled with the spirit of Yahweh, this ruler will bring justice to the poor and the oppressed, and his word alone will be fatal to evildoers and tyrants.

In this way, Isaiah gives the first sketch of the future figure who will later be identified by the stereotyped term 'Messiah'. This picture is very closely related to his encounter with God and the proclamation to which he is driven on the basis of that encounter. It is with justification that Isaiah is called the prophet of faith. Thanks to the many words which his disciples recorded, we can see the truths of comments which Fr Renckens makes elsewhere. 'The prophets who have to preach the collapse of the framework of the nation have to issue a call to a personal decision of faith, and they begin to lay stress on personal responsibility.' He goes on to point out that they had first to detach themselves from the security of anonymous membership of the collective body. 'Thus the collapse of the national framework drives people towards what is personal and inward, and this in turn opens their eyes to the inadequacy of the national framework.'

Jeremiah was present at this collapse. In the book of the Bible which preserves so many of his sayings, we hear a constant repetition of the two classical themes of prophecy: protest against idolatry and protest against social injustice. They are combined in the famous indictment of Temple worship which almost cost him his life: 'Steal, murder, commit adultery, swear falsely, run after Baals – and then come and worship Yahweh in the Temple and imagine that you are safe there!'[83] That is why the Temple is going to be destroyed.

Jeremiah does not seem to think in world-wide terms. It is in keeping with his character that he seeks the universal as it were in the depths of man. He touches on it when he describes the workings of 'the heart', man's innermost being, from which all his thoughts and actions issue. There is no great portrait of the Messiah in his book, but there is the expectation of an entirely new relationship between Yahweh and his people, one that is no longer dependent on external structures because it is rooted in the hearts of men.

The universalistic character of belief in Yahweh is expressed most impressively during the exile by the prophets whose words are contained in Isaiah 40–55. The theme of social injustice no longer needs to be discussed: the old social structures no longer exist, and the deportation to Babylon has reduced all the Judaeans to the same level. The prophet is speaking to people who, in spite of everything, are struggling to believe that Yahweh has not broken with his people and means to make a new beginning. The prophet wants to strengthen this belief, and does so by his proclamation of a new exodus, a definitive version of the first exodus from Egypt. The saving intervention in which Yahweh will restore his defunct people to life will convincingly show the whole world his true nature. 'All flesh', that is, all mankind, will behold his salvation, and every knee will bow before him to the very ends of the earth.

This is an eloquent expression of the concern of Israel's God for all mankind. But a further development was necessary to arrive at the situation in which Jesus developed the ancient faith to the full.

3. The crisis of separatism

We have already met Ezra as 'the father of Judaism'. Without his zeal the Jewish community would have been overwhelmed by outside influences and ultimately would have been swallowed up in 'the melting pot of Hellenism'. In that case there would have been no possibility of a Jesus of Nazareth, or of a Bible. So it is important for anyone reading the Bible to consider this period carefully. We shall begin by looking at the emphasis on separatism to be found in the book of Deuteronomy.

This law book belongs to the time of the national revival in Judah under king Josiah (about 640–609 BC). A century earlier, powerful Israel had been destroyed by the Assyrians, and this was seen as Yahweh's punishment for Israel's alliance with the local Baals. If Judah were to have a future, every trace of this pagan religion had to be rooted out, and everyone who was involved in it or encouraged it had to be removed, without pity, from the national community. The law book urged total loyalty and love towards Yahweh. He was to be loved and trusted with all men's soul and all their strength, and pure worship was to be offered to him in one place only. The reference here is to the Temple in Jerusalem, but because the law book is attributed to Moses, the city could not be identified by name.

Because of its stress on the need to turn to Yahweh, the law book pays a great deal of attention to the welfare of others, especially those without rights: the poor, widows, orphans and foreigners. It even urges kind treatment of animals. But in order to make loyalty to Yahweh secure, it also lays down the strictest regulations for the punishment of those who are guilty of worshipping other gods or who encourage others to do so. Because of the fiction that Moses gave these laws, it has to be supposed that Israel has not yet arrived in Canaan. Hence the command to put all the cities of the land to the ban, in other words to destroy all their inhabitants: 'that they may not teach you to do according to all their abominable practices which they have done in the service of their gods, and so to sin against the Lord God'.[84]

This is the spirit in which, during the reign of Josiah, the great national epic contained in the books of Joshua, Judges, Samuel and Kings was composed. The most strongly idealized part of it is the conduct of Joshua. In the conquest he is supposed to have done what Moses had prescribed and to have killed all the inhabitants of the conquered cities. It is good to know that this did not really happen, and that what we have here are all 'stories in sermon form'.

The influence of Deuteronomy can be clearly seen in the rules which are described in Ezra 9 and 10: all the women of non-Jewish extraction together with their children are expelled from the community. However, it would be wrong to portray the further development of the Jewish faith as an intensification of this religious separatism. Other ideas were current; other texts were read which had a broader vision, like the stories from the Yahwist and the words of Deutero-Isaiah, while new books were added. Job and his friends, whom Yahweh addressed personally, are pagans; they do not belong to Israel. And in Proverbs 8 Wisdom, represented as a woman, is concerned from creation onwards with the happiness of all mankind.

The attractive short story about Ruth could be meant as a protest against Ezra's regulations. The heroine is a woman from Moab, the member of a nation from which no one might ever be admitted to the community of Yahweh. The author depicts her as a very noble woman, and makes her the ancestress of no less a figure than king David. The impressive short story about Jonah also seems to have been written as sharp condemnation of the prevailing mentality. The pagan members of the ship's crew are sympathetic and god-fearing, and the inhabitants of Nineveh promptly do what the Israelites have never done: they repent sincerely as soon as a prophet tells them to do so. The only repellent figure in the story is Jonah, the embodiment of the narrow-mindedness and self-interest which have become characteristic of the Jewish community. He tries to evade his call to proclaim salvation to the heathen and gets very cross when Yahweh does not destroy them. The skilful author of this story reaches his climax when he makes the prophet express his exasperation in one of the most appealing formulations of Israel's faith: 'I knew it! I knew that you are a gracious God, merciful, long-suffering and abundant in pity!'[85] Jonah finds the very idea of a God who cares for people outside his own nation so intolerable that he asks to be allowed to die. A sharper criticism of Jewish separatism can hardly be imagined.

Yet other Jews chose the prophetic style to express their belief in God's purpose to bring salvation to the whole world. So we have the familiar vision of the Temple mountain to which all nations will come at the end of time to learn from Yahweh how to live with one another: they will then refashion all their weapons into instruments of prosperity and peace. It is highly significant that this rapt vision was incorporated into two collections of prophetic sayings: Isaiah 2 and Micah 4. A text with a universalistic application was also added to the earlier sayings contained in Isaiah 19: Egypt and Assyria, those arch-enemies of earlier times, will turn to Yahweh in a spirit of brotherhood and Israel will become a third partner in this covenant, a blessing in the midst of the earth. The way in which expressions from the terminology of covenant and election, normally used to describe Israel as God's own people, are here applied to the two great oppressors of former times, gives this saying a special cutting edge: 'Yahweh shall say, "Blessed Egypt, *my people*; Assyria, *the work of my hands*; *Israel, my inheritance!*" '

To supplement these texts from the Bible I should like also to refer to what Renckens wrote about the great significance of the period after Ezra, the Jewish period of biblical history. It is under-standable, he says, that our sympathies are with the warm and human figures of the prophets and their deep and universalistic views. We have less feeling for a religious experience which gave the Law such a central position and which seems to us to be a form of pernicious rigorism. Consequently it is well to remember that these were the centuries in which believers produced the Old Testament, in both its Hebrew version and its Greek translation. Judaism should be seen as a first step towards realizing the 'remnant' which the prophets had foretold, the remnant with whom Yahweh would continue his pur-pose after the destruction of the mass of the nation. In the eyes of the Jews of this period this remnant would consist of humble men, a 'poor' people, poor not only in material things but above all in the religious awareness that they not only had lost all earthly possessions and supports, but could not put any trust in them anyway. Their refuge could only be Yahweh himself. To quote Fr Renckens again:

> In his everyday faithfulness to the Law, the Jew experiences his poverty, that is, his utter surrender to his God. Far from securing for himself a human guarantee of salvation through strict fulfil-ment of the Law, by that very obedience he confesses that God himself is his only support. For him, the Law is everything, be-cause it is the summation of God's way to man and therefore man's only way to God. Thus minor regulations become import-ant, and can be readily fulfilled. In glorying in the Law of Yahweh, the Jew glories in faith. The national collapse which robbed the Jew of every human support and literally made him poor also became, through faith, a divine experience. What had been a national disaster was understood, in faith, as a gracious judgment of the God who, in the act of withdrawing himself, maintains a remnant of believers and comes near to them.[86]

So the Jewish writings in the Bible, i.e. the books which were com-posed during the Jewish period, and those which are preserved only in the Septuagint, must not be read in the nationalistic and legalistic spirit in which they were later understood, but in terms of the spirit in which they were written.

Fr Renckens describes the later spirit in this way: 'Official Judaism

130

in the time of Christ had forgotten the spirit in which it had been born and had gradually come to look for all too human a guarantee of salvation, in all kinds of external observances, and in a racist attitude.' We have tried to understand this attitude as a consequence of the struggle forced on the Maccabees and the sacrifices that they made. It is clear that from that time on Jews thought in completely negative terms about the other nations, who were then united in the Hellenistic world. Loyal Jews saw this world as the declared enemy of their community, and their community as God's only domain on earth. Of the four beasts which Daniel sees rising out of the sea, the last is the most dreadful.

In Jesus' time, then, the view prevailed among Jews that there was no hope for other nations. Only the faithful observance of the Law could give any prospect of a future with God. That was the official teaching. However, not all the rabbis were entirely comfortable with this view. The American scholar W. D. Davies has spoken in this connection of an 'uneasy conscience'.[87] He sees evidence of this in the variety of views about proselytism. There were Jews who, as Jesus says in the gospel of Matthew, 'cross sea and land in order to gain a single convert'. They believed that a Gentile had a chance to survive only if he was incorporated as fully as possible into the chosen people and, as it were, took on Jewish nationality. According to a rabbi from the beginning of the second century, God had scattered the Jews among the nations with precisely this aim, that they should make as many proselytes as possible. However, all rabbis did not share this view, and the attitude of some of the proselytes was equivocal, to say the least. In any case, it is quite untrue that in the time of Jesus the heathen were simply written off so completely that there was no point in even discussing them.

There were discussions. This is evident from the theories put forward to prove that the other nations had been given the same chance as Israel. If they were in this hopeless condition, it was their own fault. One of the arguments was that at one time on Sinai God had offered the Law to all nations. Only Israel had accepted his gift; everyone else had rejected the offer and had thus forfeited their only chance of salvation.

Alongside this, the theory developed that God had also sent prophets to the Gentiles. There were those who took the figure of

Balaam in the book of Numbers as a starting point and told how he was sent as a prophet to the Gentiles, just as Moses was sent as a prophet to Israel. He turned into seven prophets in the tradition, all of whom were rejected by heathen nations.

So when Jesus made his appearance, the Jewish community was already familiar with what might be called a 'Gentile problem'. And there is every reason to suppose that this was the real problem with which that zealous Pharisee called Saul was wrestling in his Jewish environment.

Because the conviction that Jews were different was more deeply rooted in Paul than among the Galileans whom Jesus had gathered round him as a nucleus, Paul was also much more keenly aware of the way in which Jesus had abolished the separatism by allowing all men without distinction to share in Israel's privilege. So the rest of Paul's life was taken up with world-wide activity in which he sought to create everywhere those radiating centres of the universal 'family of God' which Jesus had in view.

If we refer back to the outline of Jesus' ministry in the first chapter, we might summarize what has been said in the last few pages rather like this. At the root of Israel's religion lay the experience of the divine as personal, as an appeal to and an offer of fellowship. This implied universality. But the Jews felt the need to stress their distinctiveness from all other people. Hence, in the centuries after the exile, the increasing tension between the all-embracing principle of their religion and its actual realization. Jesus appeared at the climactic point of this tension. He experienced it to the point of death. So he was seen as the embodiment of the appeal that is called 'God', and hence as the nucleus of a universal human community.

4. Inspiration for 'a new confessionalism'

'It all sounds much too modern for me, and above all it smacks too much of humanism.' 'Doesn't this whole approach to Israelite religion and to the work of Jesus involve reading too much into the text?' Some people will undoubtedly object along these lines. Of course I would concede that there is some reading in. No one can look at the past otherwise than through his own eyes, or rather, from the perspective of his own time, which he cannot avoid. I am also very conscious of what a biblical scholar – an Anglo-Saxon, of course – identified in a book title as *The Peril of Modernizing Jesus*.[88] But as a real answer I want to point to the fact that the first generations of believers accepted and experienced Christianity in precisely this way: as a belief that founded a fellowship. This has recently been emphasized once again by classical scholars who have studied the rapid spread of Christianity. In 1961, the Dominican scholar A. J. Festugière, an expert on the many religious tendencies in the world of the time, concluded a short study of ancient Greek popular religion with this personal comment:

> If I may tell you my own feelings, the feelings of a dyed-in-the-wool historian who has reflected endlessly on the mysterious transition from Greek paganism to the Christian faith, I would say this: that what caused these pagans to be converted was not so much the novelty of the doctrine that was proclaimed to them as the Christian example of mutual love and the impression that converts received when they joined the Christian community. At last someone loved them; at last they were no longer alone … It was this that was totally new about Christianity. It was this that touched men's hearts and converted them. Not the word, but the example. Or rather, the truth of the word as demonstrated by the example. The sublimities of doctrine usually went over people's heads, as they do today. But the untiring love for neighbours, this they saw, and in this they shared.[89]

The English scholar E. R. Dodds agrees with this view. The perspective from which he writes is rather different from that of Festugière. In his masterly study of the relationship between pagans and Christians in this early period, he confesses to having no personal convictions at all. His book is surprisingly matter of fact. When at the end of it he discusses some of the psychological advantages which furthered the growth of the Christian faith and contributed to its victory, he names as the last and most prominent one the influence of Christian communal life.

> Modern social studies have brought home to us the universality of the 'need to belong' and the unexpected ways in which it can influence human behaviour, particularly among the rootless in-

habitants of great cities. I see no reason to think that it was otherwise in antiquity: Epictetus has described to us the dreadful loneliness that can beset a man in the midst of his fellows. Such loneliness must have been felt by millions – the urbanised tribesman, the peasant come to town in search of work, the demobilised soldier, the rentier ruined by inflation, and the manumitted slave. For people in that situation membership of a Christian community might be the only way of maintaining their self-respect and giving their life some semblance of meaning. Within the community there was human warmth: some one was interested in them, both here and hereafter. It is therefore not surprising that the earliest and the most striking advances of Christianity were made in the great cities – in Antioch, in Rome, in Alexandria. Christians were in a more than formal sense 'members of one another'; I think that was a major cause, perhaps the strongest single cause, of the spread of Christianity.[90]

Thus our description of what Jesus actually had in mind is no modern, humanistic interpretation. It is true that these experts on early Christianity make it clear to us that the *conceptions* of the faith in this first period differed from what is possible today. A clear recognition of this fact seems to me to be of the utmost importance for our ecumenical endeavours.

We have seen that the gospels give us a portrait of Jesus which is also a particular interpretation. There he is understood and portrayed in a biblical manner; he is 'biblicized', and that in a way that could speak to people of the Greco-Roman world. This way has become foreign to us. To take one example, it was not the human attributes of Jesus which impressed those to whom the gospel came to be preached. In their eyes he was first of all the Son of God manifest among men, announced in advance by prophecy, performing numerous miracles, and after his death taken up into glory. Another expert on early Christianity, A. D. Nock, writes that for this period Jesus is

a saviour rather than a pattern, and the Christian way of life is something made possible by Christ the Lord through the community rather than something arising from the imitation of Jesus. The central idea is that of divinity brought into humanity

134

to complete the plan of salvation, not that of perfect humanity manifested as an inspiration ... The personal attractiveness of Jesus had done much to gather the first disciples, though even then the impression of power was probably more important than the impression of love; thereafter the only human qualities which proved effective were those of individual Christian teachers and disciples.[91]

Thus for Nock, too, it is the human qualities of Christians which exert this power of attraction, not those of Jesus himself. He was esteemed above all for his divine qualities. No doubt profound statements about him will go over the heads of many people, as Festugière assumed. There is even a comment in the New Testament, in the 'Second Letter of Peter', that there are difficult passages in Paul's letters. All this affects the interpretation of Jesus' person and work.

Now it seems to me that a line can be drawn from this point to the separated Christian churches, each with its own 'confession'. Once the persecutions were over and the Christian movement was formalized into an officially recognized religion, people had time and opportunity to bring together the conceptions in the New Testament, i.e. its still unco-ordinated interpretations of Jesus, and to fix them in systematic dogmatic formulations, dogmas. I know that I am generalizing rather wildly. But I would still like to ask whether the later separation of the Christian churches is not to some extent a result of divergent and contrasting elaborations of these dogmas.

If what I have said is true, then a carefully thought out historical approach to the Bible should lead to even better relationships between the churches than have been achieved so far. Such an approach can explain the real aims of Jesus, and can do so in such a way that they can be expressed in simple language. In so doing it shows the relative character of dogmatic formulations, which by their very nature have a divisive effect. This should allow the churches to concentrate all their energies on giving heed to a summons which Christians regard as a divine summons, grounded in the need of their fellow men. In our time this need extends to the whole of humanity, which is threatened with destruction. Faith in Jesus calls for collaboration with all others who, regardless of who or where they may be, are involved in furthering the common life of humanity and giving it an on-going perspective. In his own distinctively terse style, the Roman Catholic philosopher F. Tellegen recently wrote about *the new type of confessionalism that is now in the making.* In his view 'it must be developed in such a way that Christian believers, non-believers and those of other faiths can see its effect and experience it as a contribution to the solution of the most vital human question.'[92] By means of this new form of confessionalism the message of salvation can enter into present-day history and become effective in it as long as two conditions are fulfilled. The first of these is that the claim of Christians to possess the only true faith should be relativized, in both words and actions. The second is that this confessionalism should give priority to human co-operation, to current problems and working together on them.

Furthermore, this new form of confessionalism must be dynamic and flexible, and must not mark out or retain for itself any special territory. 'Activity in connection with current problems is in principle the task of all men, and involves teamwork and collaboration. Christians, as those with a message of salvation, have no authority at all to encroach upon this right. Like anyone else, they must see what needs to be done by human beings here and now. But they should also be aware how the message of salvation can be meaningful in such teamwork, and how Christians can function in it.' Christians need to spell this out in every new situation. There are no firm rules. 'The new confessionalism will have to be a manifest service to all mankind. It must be carried on by inspired and inspiring Christians, who are just as flexible as our own changed world.'

In this view, Christians have no special contribution to make in terms of *content* when they collaborate with others in the service of mankind. Their unique contribution is their motivation, the inspiration they bring. For them this lies in the person whose name they bear, Christ, one of the titles of the man from Nazareth who was called Jesus.

Now it seems to me to be extremely important, in connection with any view of his person as a source of inspiration, to remember his own actions and the motivation which lay behind his own work. In his life he wanted to express what our portrait of him identified as God's concern for the founding of communities. He took up the cause of those who had been expelled from God's community, the sinners. He steadfastly persisted in this attitude, making God's nature visible and tangible, even when he knew that that would cost him his life. Shortly before his death he expressed this during his last meal with his disciples. In his actions over bread and wine he summed up what motivated him, the significance he attached to the death that would consummate his human life and through which, so to speak, he would begin to belong to the past, or would pass into history. By means of this gesture of self-giving in the form of bread and wine he created the possibility of continuing to be active in history through the determinative feature of his life, the summons to men to form a community.

We must remember that after Jesus' death, his disciples did not get any new historical information about him. The mysterious experiences that they had afterwards assured them that in Jesus God was still addressing himself to men. This faith penetrated their lives so deeply, and had such powerful effects, that they saw the Spirit of God at work there. They felt that working of the Spirit when they were describing and explaining all that they had experienced with Jesus. It was interpretation, translation, explanation of a period of history which was past once and for all. The author of the Fourth Gospel seems to have put on Christ's own lips a forecast of what the Holy Spirit would do after his departure: he would make the disciples remember what Jesus had said to them and would show them the meaning of his ministry, his life and his death for mankind.

As I have already said, the interpretations given in later Christian doctrine arose out of the interpretations preserved in the New Testament. In due course there were doctrines of the Trinity, the incarnation, redemption, the sacraments, the church and of many other aspects of Christianity. These diverse elaborations of doctrine played a part in causing divisions in Christianity over the following centuries: splinter groups developed alongside and in opposition to one another, thus obscuring the message which they claimed to embody. Furthermore, these elaborate doctrines and doctrinal formulas have come to mean less and less to people of modern times. For a great many Christians, what the churches preach no longer has any connection with the world of their experience.

This is why I think that it is vitally important for the church's proclamation to refer back to that closed period of history with which the first disciples also had to come to terms, after Jesus' death. For that is concerned with actual people who came together, were involved in all kinds of relationships and also found themselves at odds with one another. Anyone, anywhere who shares his life with others will know what this means.

Most Christians, however, do not have such an affinity with some of the interpretations of the Jesus event. A number of New Testament authors found it a meaningful explanation of Jesus' significance for mankind to say that on the cross he paid the price for our sins once and for all and that he then achieved our redemption by means of his blood. Perhaps the more elaborate doctrines of the atonement developed in later centuries meant something to the people of the time. But in our modern age many Christians are asking quite openly, 'What does it mean to say that I have been redeemed on the cross? What can I sense of that now?'

In the first centuries of the church believers could see what redemption meant. They came into a community which was characterized by, or at least strove for, mutual respect and love and untiring service. This seemed to be the kind of redemption that Jesus brought. In his spirit, something was realized in the church of the common life of 'God's family' as Jesus had intended it. In our time, Christian believers, non-believers and those of other faiths will have to be able to 'see and experience the effect of our confession as a contribution towards solving the most pressing questions of mankind', as Tellegen put it. And it seems to me that the inspiration for doing this can constantly be furthered by the preaching of Jesus, and by understanding Jesus as he really lived and worked among us men.

5. No biblical proofs for faith

Now what can be the function of the Bible in this new form of confessionalism? Here we come up against the very difficult question of its authority. Previously, the authority of the Bible was thought to lie in the miraculous history which it told, and which was supposed to bear a divine guarantee. It is worth looking into the question here.

The 'old' confessions were characterized by a concern to provide a pure expression of the truth of faith. The impression was sometimes given that this truth could be proved, certainly in Roman Catholic circles. In the nineteen thirties, when I was in secondary school, I was taught religious education from an apologetics book, a defence of the Catholic faith in three parts. During my theological training, this book was replaced by hefty manuals in Latin which provided even more detailed proofs. We began with the existence of God. Then followed the proof that he can reveal himself, then that he has done so, and on things went in this way up to and including the proof that the church of Rome is the only true church of Christ. I do not know how things were in Protestant circles, but I have been assured that apologetic proofs of this kind were also customary in strict Calvinist churches. When in the second chapter we considered reactions from the orthodox side to the historical approach, we in fact saw points of agreement in the ways in which it was rejected both by the teaching authority of Rome and by defenders of traditional Protestant belief.

An important link in the chain of proofs I mentioned above was provided by the miracles and the fulfilments of prophecy recorded in the Bible. A miracle was defined as an event which cannot come about through natural forces. Sometimes the definition went like this: a miracle is an interruption of the regular course of nature; now only God himself can break the laws of nature that he has established; if a man performs such a miracle he can do so only by the power of God; therefore everything that he says must also bear the weight of divine authority. Moreover, knowledge of the future is reserved for God. If someone announces long in advance an event which takes place later, this is proof that he received his foreknowledge directly from God.

Nowadays these proofs will no longer do. They are regarded as irrelevant, invalid and even misleading. Of the many factors which have led to this development, I shall mention only three.

First is the idea that *faith and proof are mutually exclusive*. Belief lies on a different plane from insights and certainties that can be proved. Belief is on the level of personal relationships. Love between two people is based on choice and self-surrender; these lie outside the realm of proof. In a good marriage, husband and wife have no need of proofs of mutual love. Of course such love needs to be expressed, but the presupposition is that each loves the other. As soon as something goes wrong between them so that they lose faith in each other, no expression by the one can serve to prove to the other that he or she is really loved. Even the most expensive present cannot restore the relationship. It can be interpreted by the one who has lost faith as a manoeuvre, whatever the intention may be. As long as this other person has no trust, he or she cannot be convinced by any gesture.

From the time of the prophet Hosea onwards, it cannot be called irreverent to describe biblical faith in terms of human love, not even in terms of that intensified form that we call being in love. When I am giving instruction in the faith I like to point to three elements in love which go to explain the faith of Israel. Love just comes over a person; it gives him or her a new view of everything, of both the beloved and the world; and there is no way of expressing it in appropriate words, let alone of proving it.

Thus Israel bears witness that this special relationship with God has come over it. The initiative is always on his side. Abraham suddenly hears the voice calling him. God suddenly appears in Moses' life when Moses is unsuspectingly looking after his sheep near a bush. And this sort of thing happens again and again over the course of Israel's history; it gives Israel a view of God unlike that of any other people. Israel saw him as an all-embracing power, gracious and merciful. The people saw him at work in creation, in history and in everything that happened. Whereas others would say that the Assyrians were making plans to launch a campaign against Syria and Palestine, believing Israelites would say that their God had summoned Assyrian armies against Palestine. Others could hardly understand what was said of Yahweh by prophets and lawgivers and leaders about his commands and his world-encompassing promises, or their communal confessions of faith in their prayers and their songs of praise. No Israelite could prove to anyone outside this community of faith that his experience was one of the most profound reality and was concerned with the loftiest truth.

I then usually try to show how these features can also be seen in the faith of Jesus' first disciples, and in that of the later church. When a large number of groups within a religion that has gained widespread acceptance over the centuries have produced a wealth of expressions of their faith, they can develop into a system of truths which are claimed as revelation, regardless of the fact that they stem from the language of love, and that they are both inadequate and unprovable.

The second factor is the increasing conviction that there must be an explanation for every phenomenon in this world, and that such an explanation will be found at some time or another. It is true that natural scientists are less optimistic about the potentiality of their work than were their colleagues of a century ago, but the fact remains that this conviction has become a common assumption among the people of our Western world, and for them miracle stories cannot be proof of divine intervention.

The third factor is the historical study of the Bible. This study has shown that the biblical accounts of marvellous events and of predictions which came true were not meant as factual reporting. They seem to be one of the forms in which the people of the Bible expressed their faith, a way of sharing in what it meant, in 'celebrating' and in handing it on to succeeding generations. Because this point is so important for people who read the Bible in our time, I shall go into it in a little more detail.

A few pages ago I referred to the military campaigns of the Assyrians. They seem to me to illustrate clearly the point I am making here. We know a good deal about Assyrian culture and history at the time of Isaiah. Although there are gaps in our knowledge of the campaigns which Tiglath-Pileser and his successors carried on in 'the West', we can be sure that they were purely secular events. It has always been possible in principle to know why the Assyrian kings undertook them, how they were organized, and what results they produced. No doubt the diplomats in Jerusalem were quite well informed themselves. Yet Isaiah says that it is Yahweh who has brought the Assyrians into action. He has 'given them the signal' to march into Judah and destroy it.

Isaiah sees a tangible event, which can be understood in its own terms, as an action on the part of Yahweh. What happens to Israel is part of its inter-relationship with God. God addresses himself to his people through events, and his spokesman, the prophet, discloses what they mean.

A biblical narrative could well have taken the following form: 'The king of Assyria was lying fast asleep. Suddenly his room was filled with a heavenly light. An angel of the Lord appeared to him, awakened him and said, "O king, assemble your army and march to the land of Judah and to its capital city Jerusalem. For thus says the

Lord: I have seen the sins of my people and I am sending you to punish them . . ."'

This story does not happen to appear in the Bible. But there are many others which have a similar background: a belief that God is at work in particular events, and which expresses this by telling of an angel whom he has sent, a natural phenomenon that he causes to happen, or in some other way. When we looked at the books of Chronicles we saw how the author introduced new miracles into an old story to make it express his belief more clearly. The ten plagues which in Exodus are said to have come upon Egypt are the result of a combination of earlier stories. An analysis of Exodus 14 shows that the earliest nucleus of this text did not describe the passage through the Red Sea as a miracle. An east wind pushed the shallow water back so that the fleeing Semitic slaves were able to escape their pursuers, who were stuck in the morass and drowned when the wind changed. An Egyptian who escaped drowning could have said: 'That bunch had a bit of good luck and we had bad luck' (though in passing we may note that this would have been unlikely because Egyptians were believers too; they also saw the hand of their gods in events of any importance). In the light of Moses' faith, the event became significant as a revelation of God's saving nature. As Hendrikus Berkhof, a leading Dutch Protestant theologian, puts it, the crossing of the sea 'is usually presented as the central revelatory event on which the faith of Israel has lived down the centuries. This is not incorrect, as long as we see that the event in itself did not have a revelatory character; it acquired this by virtue of the context in which it was experienced.'[93]

These examples ought to be enough. However, there is one thing that ought to be emphasized. In antiquity, a notable or striking phenomenon, one that made a difference to life, could more easily be seen as an act of God than we moderns tend to imagine. People did not react by looking for a natural explanation. Their concern to understand precisely what had happened was not as strong, and the concept of nature as a system of forces governed by laws was quite unknown.

We must remember this above all when we come to the miracles in the gospels. Anyone who takes a truly historical approach will avoid using the word miracle by itself and will talk instead about the

142

miracle *stories* of the gospels. When we analyse them, a great variety emerges. A few of them are entirely or partially 'symbolic': one might think of the changing of water into wine at Cana or the raising of Lazarus, both of which occur in the Fourth Gospel. In other miracle stories the meaning of the miracle has clearly had an effect on the way in which it is told. Here I am thinking of a point which we found Origen discussing: anyone who believes in Christ experiences his spiritual power which can heal inward blindness, the leprosy of sin, and so on. However, close analysis will bring us to the fact that people remembered how Jesus was involved in a number of miraculous healings. Suppose that some men of our time had been there then: perhaps they would have explained these miracles in what we call 'psycho-somatic' terms, i.e. the influence that deep internal disturbances can have on the state of the body and its organs. However, we just cannot transport modern men back to the time of Jesus, and in any case, their 'explanation' would not have been relevant then. What Berkhof said about the revelatory character that an event acquires 'through the context in which it was experienced' applies here in a very special way. Anyone who met Jesus and was open with him discovered a deeper dimension in what he said and did. On one occasion Jesus himself had pointed to this when he referred to the men of Nineveh in the story of Jonah and to the visit of the queen of Sheba: 'Behold, a greater than Jonah is here, a greater than Solomon is here.' When Jesus drove out evil spirits which tormented men, they indeed felt that, as Jesus put it, the 'finger of God' was at work. Once again, though, you had to be open to him if you wanted to discover this. Those who kept themselves closed certainly recognized that he was doing supernatural acts. But according to their derogatory comments, these came from 'Beelzebub, the prince of the devils'. Others said that he had been taught by Egyptian sorcerers.

Mark writes that Jesus could do no miracles in Nazareth because the people there did not believe in him. Further on, he notes that Jesus refused to accede to the Pharisees' demand that he should give them a 'sign from heaven' as proof of his mission. They were asking for the impossible. Even the most expensive present is meaningless to the wife who has lost faith in her husband.

The story of the fulfilment of a prophecy can no more serve as proof than can the story of a miracle. It is often clearly an expression of faith. David conquered the Edomites, a kindred nation that was established earlier than Israel. A conviction that this conquest was in accordance with the plans of Yahweh led to the making of a story in which God spoke to Rebecca while she was with child: this story contained a prophecy to her that of her future sons Jacob (Israel) and Esau, the elder would serve the younger. Similarly, the Israelites felt that living in the land of Canaan was a gift from Yahweh. They expressed this in the form of a promise from God to the patriarchs. Where we are told of promises made by God to Abraham, Isaac and Jacob, we are dealing with expressions of faith.

We find a real prediction in Jeremiah 28. The prophet said to Hananiah on divine authority: 'Before the year is out, you will die.' And that is what happened. For Baruch, who recorded this, it was undoubtedly a proof that Jeremiah was a true prophet. But his enemies might have given a different explanation, for instance, that Hananiah had not been looking very well recently.

Earlier on, I mentioned the important role played by the 'messianic prophecies' in the preaching of the early church. It is clear that these, too, can no longer serve as proofs for us. Some believers are shocked by this and feel themselves robbed of their old certainties. Others value the positive consequences. Here is one of them.

In earlier times, proofs for the truth of Christianity were presented so thoroughly that it seemed that those who did not accept them and remained outside the mother church must be positively malicious. A younger sister of mine seemed to have understood her religious instruction at school quite well. She happened to ask a visitor whether he was a Catholic. 'No,' he replied. Her reply was emphatic: 'In that case you will go to hell ... But what a pity! You're such a nice man!' We may laugh at that now. It was the spirit of a closed group, which limited the truth and eternal salvation to its own members. At the time there were also similar groups in the Protestant world. However, in earlier centuries such a mentality was no laughing matter for many people. When Christianity became the state religion, the official truth, and Christendom came into being, life was intolerable for those who could not accept official teaching. Here I am thinking in particular of the Jewish communities all over Europe. The accepted view was that they just had to be evil, so it was permissible to rob them, persecute them and torment them. Of course all kinds of social and economic factors soon became involved. First and foremost, however, was their resistance to 'the truth'. An American rabbi concerned with modern trends in Judaism recently wrote of the 'revolutionary changes' which Judaism has undergone in the course of its history. The first that he mentioned was the destruction of the state of Judah in 578 BC and the deportation to Babylon, and the second was the destruction of Jerusalem by the Romans in AD 70. His third revolutionary change was 'a result of the ideas which inspired the American and the French Revolutions. Long treated as an outcast in Christian society, the Jew, at last, was also to benefit from the recognition of the Rights of Man. The Ghetto walls fell. Emancipation came to the Jew in the West.'⁹⁴ This happened at the very time when people began to approach the Bible historically. We have seen quite clearly how strong the opposition of orthodox groups was to this approach.

Finally, I want to say something about the divine character of the Bible. In my sketch of Jesus' preaching and the cause to which he utterly committed himself, I avoided the term 'kingdom of God'. I sincerely hope that you did not notice this, because if you did not, it would strengthen a conviction that has grown in me over the years. My feeling is that we can only communicate the faith to a great many people of our time if we replace a great many traditional terms with others which are more understandable and less portentous. We must be able to translate the concerns of Jesus into comprehensible language.

Now one of the expressions which I feel that we must avoid, at least for the time being, is the assertion that the Bible is the Word of God. It conjures up the idea that God himself wrote the Bible and also that God addresses himself directly to those who read the Bible or listen to it being read. Thinking like that is wrong. Theologians can justify the expression with a great mass of complicated arguments. But it is misleading to the ordinary believer. The Bible contains only the words of men.

Thanks to the historical approach, we have discovered how different were the expressions of those who shared the same faith. The Old Testament shows what happens to a way of living in a group which goes through history believing in one God, but in different forms of society. First there is a tribal alliance, then a kingdom (which is soon split apart) and then the unique form of Judaism, a society which is unparalleled in history. The biblical texts reflect much of what went on among people in this tradition of faith. Some of them were written on the basis of a very intimate association with this one God, as it were from the very heart of the community. We might think of Jeremiah's conversations with God *set alongside* the detailed prescriptions for worship in the book of Leviticus; or of the accounts of the national heroes in Judges and Samuel *set alongside* the wise counsels for a happy life in Proverbs; or of the ardent prayers and hymns in the book of Psalms *set alongside* the sceptical views of Ecclesiastes.

Those whose voices are heard in the Old Testament are all human, even when they say, 'Thus says Yahweh' . . . They are then expressing what they believe that God has to say to his people at that particular moment. So it is that in Jeremiah God speaks in an entirely different style, with different images and a different terminology from that in Isaiah. Jesus, too, interpreted what God had to say to his people. But he never introduced his sayings with the formula, 'Thus says Yahweh'. *God's intentions and desires were so completely his own that he did not need to make this distinction.*

The people whose voices we hear in the New Testament speak from the tradition which is based on Jesus, from within the community which developed by recognizing him as its sole Lord. In various ways they bear witness to what happens to thinking and living and coming together when all of these are dominated by faith in Jesus.

To acknowledge all this is not necessarily to see the Bible as just one more human book. Being a Christian means confessing Jesus as Lord. We recognize that the God of Israel has expressed himself fully in Jesus, and that Jesus is the climax of a tradition of faith in this God of Israel. Written words have their own place within that tradition, alongside lawgivers and prophets. So from the perspective of faith, the books of the Old Testament serve as a prelude. The first community is part of the Jesus event. That is the beginning of the tradition with which we identify ourselves when we accept Jesus as our Lord. The books of the New Testament are part of the foundations of the community which we form. That is why they are so special and so indispensable for us.

It seems to me to be wrong and misleading to suppose that the Bible was written by authors like Moses, Isaiah and Matthew, people whom God inspired, into whom he breathed, or to whom he dictated. This is wrong, because many books of the Bible were in fact the work of many anonymous authors, and from the deposit of a long tradition. Such a view is misleading, because it can so easily isolate the Bible from the highest authority for Christians, the claims and the promises of Jesus. Jesus himself was quite clear about this. And it is Matthew, who was more of a scribe than the other evangelists, who has handed down to us the most impressive picture of the Last Judgment: the judge will not ask us what we did with the Bible, but simply whether we responded positively to the word which was expressed to us in the need of the 'least of his brethren'.

6. Conclusion

Taking up a familiar Dutch proverb, one might say, 'Every believer has his favourite text.' We have come across a great many examples of the way in which people used to twist biblical texts to suit themselves. The historical approach involves our seeking what was originally meant by those responsible for the texts. We found that the essential element in Israel's experience of God was expressed in Jesus, in such a way that he could become the centre of a universal human community.

Of course our eyes are opened to this reality by the ideas and ideals of our own time, and it is the needs and distresses of our world which lead us to believe in this Jesus as the only one who can give us a future. This faith in Jesus, who shows us the meaning of God's concern to found a community, brings us together in the context of a new confessionalism. Only in this perspective can biblical texts claim any authority.

It is clear that the Bible comes in to its own in the observance of the Lord's Supper, the eucharist, in which we accept Jesus' invitation to meet one another by sharing in his table; in so doing we make a significant beginning to what must be the concern of the whole of humanity.

When we take texts to read in that setting, our attention is drawn first of all to those which express his intentions, commands and promises most clearly. This was the proclamation which involved him in the situation which we commemorate: 'On the night before he was betrayed . . .'

Stories from the gospels and passages from the other writings of the New Testament can go along with this reading, as long as they help to elucidate what Jesus wants to be for those who are present. This must be much more evident in the use of passages from the Old Testament. Here, of course, everything depends first on the degree to which those involved are familiar with the texts and themes of the Bible and the biblical way of expressing things and secondly on the degree of interest which people have in taking them further.

One basic principle should be that mystification is avoided and that a text is used only when something of its original meaning can be seen. It is not necessary that everything should always be clear. In the end, the texts are concerned with the mysteries of human existence, and the language they use is in the last resort that of faith and love.

This fact above all restrains me from giving any more definite directions and suggestions. All Christians must work together to arrive at a use of the Bible which no longer divides but unites us. And that work cannot be confined to those specialists who are up to coping with the technical difficulties of scholarship; anyone who is motivated by Jesus and his spirit must be able to join in.

Notes

In the text, Fr Grollenberg often makes his own translation of biblical quotations. Where English versions do not reflect the nuances of his rendering I have translated his words; elsewhere I have used the English texts indicated in these notes.

1. The story about the Koran can be found in G. van der Leeuw, *Phänomenologie der Religion*, Tübingen ²1956, p.500, n.1.

2. The historian is John Bright, *History of Israel*, SCM Press ²1972, p.433. For the birthday of Judaism see A. Gelin, in *Moïse, l'homme de l'Alliance*, Paris 1955, p.51.

3. The quotations are from Ecclesiasticus 24.7–23 (most English versions omit v.18), and Baruch 3.31–4.1 (Jerusalem Bible = JB).

4. I have taken these rabbinical texts about the Torah from E. Schürer, *Die Geschichte des jüdischen Volkes im Zeitalter Jesu Christi*, Leipzig ⁴1907, pp.365f., and W. Bousset, *Die Religion des Judentums im späthellenistischen Zeitalter*, Tübingen ³1926, p.121.

5. The Book of Jubilees is translated in R. H. Charles, *The Apocrypha and Pseudepigrapha of the Old Testament*, Oxford University Press 1913, Vol. II, pp.1–82. The Isaac quotation comes from 26.34.

6. The text of Exodus 21.22f. is discussed by T. Beemer in a study of 'Abortus provocatus en de waarde van het menselijk leven', *Tijdschrift voor Theologie* 10, 1970, pp.280f.

7. There is an English translation of the Letter of Aristeas in Charles, *Apocrypha and Pseudepigrapha* II, pp.83–122; the quotation comes from §307. The introduction refers to the development of the legend, beginning with Philo. His version is in his *Life of Moses* ii, 5–7.

8. The Septuagint = 'seventy' is so-called because in the story of the giving of the Law, seventy elders accompany Moses up the mountain, and these were seen as suitable recipients for the Greek version. Seventy-two represents six members from each of the twelve tribes.

9. F. Weinreb, *De Bijbel als schepping*, Den Haag 1963, pp.331 and 345.

10. Aristeas, §§139ff.

11. The quotation comes from Philo's work *On the Posterity of Cain*. The English translation follows the long extract given by C. K. Barrett, *The New Testament Background: Selected Documents*, SPCK 1957, pp.180–2.

12. Philo's interpretation of the three patriarchs is described in J. Daniélou, *Philon d'Alexandrie*, Paris 1957, pp.138ff.

13. C. Siegfried's twenty-three rules are listed by F. Schröger, *Der Verfasser des Hebräerbriefes als Schriftausleger*, Regensburg 1968, pp.293–301.

14. This book appears as IV Ezra in Charles, *Apocrypha and Pseudepigrapha* II, pp.542–624.

15. Translations of the commentaries on Habakkuk and Psalm 37 are taken from G. Vermes, *The Dead Sea Scrolls in English*, Penguin Books 1962, pp.239, 243.

16. The quotation is from the English translation of Joseph Klausner, *Jesus of Nazareth*, Allen and Unwin 1925, p.376. My attention was drawn to it years ago in a book by C. H. Dodd, who has recently used it again in *The Founder of Christianity*, Fount Books 1973, p.89.

17. The quotation comes from I Maccabees 4.46 (Revised Standard Version = RSV); see also 14.41.

18. The saying about the sick and the physician comes from Luke 5.31 RSV; the call of Zacchaeus the tax-collector from Luke 19.8 RSV.

19. The story of the good Samaritan comes from Luke 10.25–37; that of the rich man and his possessions from Luke 18.18–25; and that of the Roman official from Luke 7.1–10.

20. The saying about unlimited forgiveness comes from Matthew 18.21–35. For anger against one's brother see Matthew 5.21f.

21. On the sabbath being made for man, see Mark 2.27; on what makes a man unclean, see Mark 7.15 RSV.

22. The story of the woman taken in adultery has been preserved in some manuscripts of the Fourth Gospel, John 8.1–11.

23. Jesus' saying about precedence and service comes from Luke 22.24–27 RSV.

24. Peter recognizes Jesus as Messiah, Mark 8.29; there is a hint of this ecstatic mood in John 6.15. See also Acts 2.36.

25. There are illustrations from Egypt relating to Psalm 110 in my *Shorter Atlas of the Bible*, Penguin Books 1978, p.128.

26. Nathan's promises are in II Samuel 7.14; for Israel as God's son and first-born see Exodus 4.22f. Also Hosea 11.1; Isaiah 1.2; Jeremiah 3.19 RSV and the great prayer in Isaiah 63.15–64.12 JB. The text from Wisdom is 2.13–20 JB.

27. The sayings of Jesus come from Matthew 7.9–11 JB; Luke 12.49f. JB; Mark 9.19; Matthew 11.27.

28. Proverbs 8.22f. The sayings below on the love of God are from Romans 8.31f. and I John 4.7–9.

29. The prophecies of the birth of the Messiah are in Micah 5.1–3 and Isaiah 7.14.

30. Joel 3.1–5 (in some Bibles 2.28–32) is quoted in Acts 2.17–21.

31. The story of the manna appears in Exodus 16 and Numbers 11; of Elisha in II Kings 5.42–44, of Jesus in Mark 6.30–44; 8.1–8. The stilling of the storm comes from Mark 4.35–41 and the transfiguration from Luke 9.28–36.

32. The darkness at noon is mentioned in Amos 8.9f.

33. The curse on anyone who hangs on a tree occurs in Deuteronomy 21.23 and is cited by Paul in Galatians 3.13. The allusion to Isaiah 49 is in Galatians 1.15.

34. For Abraham's faith see Romans 4.9–12 and 17–22.

35. Romans 8.17. The text below from Genesis 12.7 is used in Galatians 3.16.

36. For the two sons of Abraham see Galatians 4.21–31. The threshing ox from Deuteronomy 25.4 is mentioned in I Corinthians 9.9.

37. James 2.20–26 RSV.

38. Paul, speaking about the veil worn by Moses, in II Corinthians 3.4–17.

39. Paul, on our knowledge of God, in I Corinthians 13.8–12.

40. The quotation is from Beryl Smalley, *The Study of the Bible in the Middle Ages*, Blackwell 1952, p.14. The sermon following can most easily be found in the edition published in Sources Chrétiennes: *Origène, Homélies sur l'Exode*, Paris 1947, pp.98ff., which has Latin and French texts. The 'prophet' quoted by Origen is Psalm 45.11.

41. I have taken over Origen's reflections on the transfiguration from H. de Lubac, *Histoire et Esprit*, Paris 1950, p.276, and from an article by J. Guillet in *Recherches de Science Religieuse* 34, 1947, p.292.

42. From the sermons on Exodus mentioned above, p.334. Origen is quoting John 15.16 and Matthew 12.29.

43. The sermons on Joshua are also to be found in Sources Chrétiennes: *Origène, Homélies sur Josué*, Paris 1960, pp.101, 118f., 341f. Origen is quoting Proverbs 26.11 or II Peter 2.22. See also Luke 11.26. The reference to the 'little children of Babylon' comes from the end of Psalm 137, and that to evil thoughts from Matthew 15.19. According to Genesis 11.9, Babel means confusion.

44. From Origen's sermons on Joshua, op. cit., pp.137f.

45. Rahab comes in Matthew 1.5; Hebrews 11.31 RSV; James 2.25.

46. The texts from Clement, Justin and Irenaeus are to be found in J. Daniélou, *Sacramentum Futuri*, Paris 1950, pp.217f. The quotation from Clement comes from I Clement 12.

47. The quotations are from H. de Lubac, op. cit., pp.207f.

48. Gregory's interpretation is taken from H. Tissot, *Les Pères vous parlent de l'Evangile*, Paris 1953, pp.686f.

49. The interpretation of the Good Samaritan follows that of L. Billot, *De Ecclesiae Sacramentis*, Rome 1931, pp.7–9.

50. J. Huizinga, *The Waning of the Middle Ages*, Edward Arnold 1924, p.187.

51. There is a rather unsatisfactory translation of this *Enarratio* in *Expositions on the Book of Psalms by St Augustine*, Vol. 3, Library of the Fathers, Parker (Oxford) 1849, pp.175ff.

52. I have quoted St Thomas from the edition of the *Opera Omnia* edited by Vivès, Vol. 18, p.228.

53. I have quoted Erasmus from a study by E. Kohls, *Die Theologie des Erasmus*, Basle 1966, pp.126f.

54. Yves Congar, 'The Sacralization of Western Society in the Middle Ages', in *Sacralization and Secularization, Concilium* 47, 1969, pp. 55–71.

55. Yves Congar, 'Ecce constitui te super gentes et regna, etc.', in the Festschrift edited by Michael Schmaus, *Theologie in Geschichte und Gegenwart*, Munich 1957, pp. 671–96. The letter of Charlemagne referred to below is quoted in J. Lecler, 'L'argument des deux glaïves', *Recherches de Science Religieuse* 21, 1931, pp.299–339.

56. The information about the use of the Bible in connection with the crusades comes from P. Rousset, *Les origines et les caractères de la première croisade*, Neuchâtel 1945.

57. The quotations come from L. Hanke, *The Spanish Struggle for Justice in the Conquest of America*, Philadelphia 1949, pp.31f., 120f.

58. I read *Het leesgezelschap van Diepenbeek* in the edition published by the Bibliotheek der Nederlandse Letteren, Amsterdam 1939.

59. My attention was called to the role of Niebuhr by S. Neill, *The Interpretation of the New Testament 1861–1961*, Oxford University Press 1964, p.7.

60. I found the statement by Lutz in an article by A. Bea, *Biblica* 40, 1959, p.325. Wellhausen's letter is in H.-J. Kraus, *Geschichte der historisch-kritischen Erforschung des Alten Testaments*, Neukirchen 1956, p.236.

61. The statement that Moses himself wrote is to be found, among other places, in Exodus 17.14; 24.4; 34.27f.; Numbers 33.2; Deuteronomy 31.19, 22. The declaration of Christ is in John 5.45–47.

62. The information about Poels is taken from the biography by J. Colsen, *Poels*, Roermond 1955, pp.85–110. Later on in the book the author describes how pressure from orthodox believers made it impossible for Poels to become professor at the Catholic University in Washington. Is it an accident that this devoted biblical scholar became the great champion of the social movement in Limburg?

63. The *Responsiones* of the Papal Biblical Commission can be found in Denziger's *Enchiridion Symbolorum*, published in a new revision every few years at Freiburg im Breisgau. This book also contains the *Motu proprio* of 18 November 1907 and the most important passages of the encylicals quoted here.

64. Aalders' book was published by J. H. Kok, Kampen.

65. The quotation comes from J. S. van der Ploeg, *Les Chants du Serviteur de Jahvé*, Paris 1936, p.16.

66. Aalders, op. cit., pp.214, 215, 218: my italics.

67. The reference here is to J. Goettsberger, *Die Bücher der Chronik oder Paralipomenon*, Bonn 1939; quotations from pp.16, 17, 159. My article 'De historiciteit der evangeliën toegelicht door het Oude Testament', *Tijdschrift voor Theologie* 4, 1964, pp.35–53, shows how the new approach to Chronicles can help in explaining the nature of the gospels.

68. *The Jerusalem Bible*, standard edition, Darton, Longman and Todd 1966, pp.492f.

69. The quotation comes from *Theologische Zeitschrift* 12, 1956, p.431. I have also used it in a detailed account of contemporary discussion of the significance of the Old Testament in *Tijdschrift voor Theologie* 2, 1962, pp.316-50.

70. Adolf von Harnack, *Marcion*, Leipzig 1921, p.127.

71. Rudolf Bultmann, 'The Significance of the Old Testament for Christian Faith', in *The Old Testament and Christian Faith*, edited by Bernhard W. Anderson, SCM Press 1964, pp.1-7.

72. L. Fonck, *Der Kampf um die Wahrheit der Heiligen Schrift seit 25 Jahren*, Innsbruck 1905, p.202.

73. The series of articles by Werner Harenberg published in *Der Spiegel* later appeared in book form: *Der Spiegel on the New Testament*, Macmillan, New York 1970; the quotations are from pp.4, 192.

74. *The Bible in Modern Scholarship*, edited by J. P. Hyatt, Abingdon Press, Nashville 1965, p.11.

75. The Scandinavian scholar referred to here is Krister Stendahl, 'The Apostle Paul and the Introspective Conscience of the West', reprinted in his *Paul among Jews and Gentiles*, SCM Press 1977, pp.78ff.

76. B. van Iersel, 'De heilshistorische betekenis van Israel', *Kosmos en Oecumene* 4, 1970, p. 315.

77. See W. McKane, *Proverbs*, SCM Press 1970, p.258.

78. R. Guardini, *Der Heilsbringer in Mythos, Offenbarung und Politik: eine theologisch-politische Besinnung*, Zurich 1946, p.10.

79. My summary follows P. Ellis, *The Yahwist*, University of Notre Dame Press, Indiana 1968.

80. Hosea 4.2.

81. Amos 9.7; 3.12 RSV.

82. J. Renckens, *De profeet van de Nabijheid Gods*, Tielt 1961, pp.158f.

83. Jeremiah 7.9.

84. Deuteronomy 20.18 RSV.

85. Jonah 4.2.

86. J. Renckens, *De godsdienst van Israel*, Roermond 1962, pp.243f.

87. W. D. Davies, *Paul and Rabbinic Judaism*, SPCK 1965, pp.63f.

88. H. J. Cadbury, *The Peril of Modernizing Jesus*, reprinted SPCK 1962.

89. A.-J. Festugière, *Revue de Théologie et de Philosophie*, 1961, p.31.

90. E. R. Dodds, *Pagan and Christian in an Age of Anxiety*, Cambridge University Press 1965, pp.137f. He refers to Festugière.

91. A. D. Nock, *Conversion*, Oxford University Press 1969, p.210.

92. F. Tellegen, in *Katholiek Artsenblad*, 1969, pp.180f.

93. H. Berkhof, in *Geloven in God*, The Hague 1970, p.124.

94. J. Petuchowsky, *Zion Reconsidered*, Twayne, New York 1966, p.8.